AGING

WITH A **LAUGH** AND A **PRAYER**

AGING

WITH A
LAUGH
AND A
PRAYER

BERNADETTE MCCARVER SNYDER

TWENTY
THIRD 23rd
PUBLICATIONS
www.23rdpublications.com

I dedicate this book to my thought-full,
ever-encouraging friend, Teresa Coyle,
who convinced me I could write this book, and to
my youth-full, ever-positive editor, Paul Pennick,
who convinced me I could get it published!

Second printing 2010

TWENTY-THIRD PUBLICATIONS
A Division of Bayard
One Montauk Avenue, Suite 200
New London, CT 06320
(860) 437-3012 or (800) 321-0411
www.23rdpublications.com

Cover image: ©istockphoto.com / YinYang

ISBN 978-1-58595-736-1
Library of Congress Catalog Card Number: 2008943612
Printed in the U.S.A.

CONTENTS

AUTHOR'S NOTE

All the stories in this book are about real people—some I have personally interviewed, some I have read about, some I have heard about through friends. I hope they all will be interesting and maybe inspiring for soon-to-be-seniors, seniors themselves, and those who live with or care for seniors.

In order to protect everyone's privacy, I chose not to use real names. So if you think one of these stories sounds familiar but the name doesn't fit, it could be the story of someone you know or it might just be the story of a senior with a similar life experience. Each story inspired a short prayer of thanksgiving for wisdom shared or insight gleaned.

I admire and am grateful to all who shared their stories with me and think their responses shed new light on this sometimes troubling, yet sometimes very joyful, "third stage of life."

Bernadette McCarver Snyder

INTRODUCTION

Who? Me? Write a book about aging? I don't know anything about that!

Well, maybe I know a little about it. Most adults know a little because they have older friends or relatives. And now I hear that soon one in five Americans will be sixty-five or over, which means there will be seventy-seven million in what is euphemistically known as the "third stage of life." It's a new Millionaire Club! And every member has a story to tell!

Maybe I wasn't listening carefully before but since I've reached the stage where I qualify for a senior discount, I've started hearing stories from people I know, have met or have heard of—and I have been inspired and enthused! Now I'm eager to share them with you.

The "senior moments" I've collected present folks of various ages who have unique approaches to the plus and minuses, perks and possibilities of aging. I hope their experiences will be "teaching moments" for you as they were for me. Their ideas just might offer a lifeline of new insights, directions, and options for dealing with this new "third stage of life." And, yes, the stories include more chuckles than tears.

Whatever stage of life you have reached, I hope you'll find this book full of ideas for accepting and appreciating each day with a laugh and a prayer.

LAUGHTER IS THE
BEST MEDICINE

A few years ago, when open-heart surgery was a relatively new procedure, Alice McGillicuddy spent some scary hours waiting while her husband, Bob, had his heart fixed. A couple of weeks after he had returned home to recover, Alice ran into a friend who had had the same surgery some time before. With a troubled look on his face, he said to Alice, "I want you to know that one of the side effects of this surgery can be depression." With one of her devilish smiles, Alice replied, "Yes, I know. I am very depressed."

Her friend's mouth dropped and he started to mumble, "I meant your husband..." but then he realized she was kidding and they both laughed. However, it is true that when one spouse has a sudden medical emergency, it has a dramatic impact on the other spouse. Life changes. It's usually a temporary change because of the need for therapy, new medicine, new diet, etc., but it can be challenging. Fortunately, Alice had a supply of laughs and a pocketful of ideas to keep Bob cheered—plus a flock of friends and family who flew in for visits, sent encouraging or humorous notes, brought in dinner, etc. In fact, with all that help, Alice and Bob were so *im*pressed, they didn't have time to be *de*pressed.

By the time most people near or reach retirement, they've had enough experience with the world to know that a few black clouds are inevitable, but those clouds often come with a bonus—the gift of understanding. Once you've survived a storm yourself, you have new sympathy for others' problems and you have the qualifications to reassure them that even black clouds keep moving and are soon gone with the wind.

Dear Lord, I know you don't have to worry about sending greeting cards but I do—birthday cards, sympathy cards, get-well cards. And I recently found one that I love to send to anyone with a solvable medical problem. On the outside, it reads, "Laughter is the best medicine" and on the inside it says, "For a small fee, I will come over and tickle you. Get well soon." Maybe they won't think it is as funny as I do but it tickles me to put that card in the mailbox. Of course, Lord, you send the best kind of greeting cards, full of hope and cheer and love, but sometimes we aren't paying attention when they come and we toss them away with the junk mail. Forgive us, Lord. Teach us to pay attention. Teach us to be aware of the messages you quietly send us every day. And please always keep us on your mailing list.

THE MAN IN THE RED HAT

Eddie Jameson always stands out in a crowd—in more ways than one. Whenever there's a special occasion, you can't miss Eddie because he will be the one wearing an Indiana-Jones style felt fedora—except Eddie's fedora is bright red! Eddie gets a kick out of wearing that red hat, but he would stand out in a crowd anyway because he's a really great guy and has had a really great life.

Eddie was working in a defense plant in New Jersey making propellers for warplanes when he got drafted and saw action in the Battle of the Bulge. After he came home and got a G.I. Bill college diploma, he took a job as a newspaper reporter, then joined a public relations/fund-raising firm and traveled all over the country. He was offered a job as director of development at a large Catholic university and became one of the university's first lay vice presidents. Whew! But he wasn't finished yet. He left the university to form his own PR firm and when he finally decided to "retire" at sixty-eight, he moved on to a rather unusual retirement job.

Since Eddie had enjoyed bachelorhood and didn't marry until he was a bit past forty, he now had a "young" family of four adult children, eight very young grandchildren, plus his charming wife, golf buddies, and lots of friends to keep him occupied, but he still needed something to "do." Searching the classified ads, he found just the job he needed. His young family was shocked when he announced that he had found a part-time job as a greeter at a funeral home!

Actually, it was a perfect fit for someone with his background. With his New Jersey accent and an Irish wit, Eddie could talk to anyone so he felt he had found a "ministry" where he could help people by offering them an understanding, empathizing presence if they needed someone to talk to or to just share a cup of coffee.

He said whenever he had left a job in the past, he liked to have something "to look forward to" and this job made him get dressed up and get out several days a week, plus he made a little extra "project money" for his left back pocket. He said some of the children he saw at the funeral home just "made his heart sing," and he has great respect for the "saints" he has met during his life.

Just recently, at age eighty-six, Eddie finally decided to retire again because he had enough other things "to look forward to." He is one of a group of volunteers who read the weekly Catholic newspaper on tape for people who have sight problems; he is the designated driver for one of his daughters who travels by wheelchair and sometimes needs a ride to work or to meet friends; he swims twice a week, likes to take his wife to matinee movies or out to dinner, has a lot of fun surprising and entertaining the grandchildren, often attends daily Mass, and always attends the monthly meetings of the local chapter of the Battle of the Bulge vets. Sounds like he's found enough to "do"—with or without the red hat—unless he starts looking at those classified ads again.

Dear Lord, the other day I heard someone talk about a "psychic" predicting the future and she said, "The only way to know the future is to plan it." Seniors don't have to do lots of long-term planning anymore like "what I'll do when I grow up," but short-term planning sounds like a good idea. If we always plan something to "do" tomorrow or next week or maybe next month, we'll always have "something to look forward to," like Eddie does. Lord, I know you have a long-term plan for me and I expect to enjoy that. Right now, though, I have lots of fun things on my short-term to-do list. Thanks, Lord, for that—and for all the doers like Eddie!

BETWIXT AND BETWEEN

Somewhere I heard the question, "If you didn't know how old you are, how old would you think you are?" So I asked Ralph Andrews that question and, after just a bit of thought, he said, "I'd be either fourteen or fifty. When I was fourteen, I was not a little kid anymore but not quite a real teenager either. I was floating in my relationship to life. I was wondering, 'What's next?' When I was fifty, I looked around and thought, 'This is OK.' I had my career and a family and enough money to pay the bills but I was between again. I was no longer a 'young adult' but not yet a real senior. And I started thinking again, 'What's next?'"

After college, Ralph started out to be a graphic artist but his interest shifted and he became a commercial photographer. He met important people, flew about on their private jets for photo shoots, and earned a very nice salary. But when his children were grown, he and his wife grew apart and divorced. He moved from a large fancy home to a small apartment where he set up a room with his photo equipment and space for the art projects that were his hobby. He had always been quiet, thoughtful, a "loner," and now a new chapter in his life began.

At one point, he took seven weeks off to go with an art study group to Florence, Italy. It was an idyllic time, being immersed in the magnificence of that art-filled city and spending time photographing the way he chose instead of with an eye to his commercial work. He began to think, "What else can I do?" After a while, although he had many clients who were happy to pay him well for his work, he decided to write and tell them all he was no longer available. After scouting about, he chose a totally new lifestyle. He became a courier, working at odd hours, delivering important papers or packages, some days around town, sometimes to other cities. And he likes it.

Today, at sixty-eight, he says he is happy, his health and finances are in good shape, and his children are all people he likes a lot. In fact, he says when he is with them, it's like visiting with old buddies. They are now on the way to fifty themselves with children of their own. So he has been surprised to suddenly find lots of little kids back in his life. And he likes that too.

He says it could be easy to see someone else's seemingly "richer" lifestyle and know you don't have that, but it's more important to see what you *do* have, and feel happy and at peace with that.

Ralph recalls growing up with only one brother and how they were always either angry at each other or laughing like crazy. As adults, the anger was gone but the humor remained. When his brother died recently, Ralph was glad his brother didn't have to suffer anymore but he misses him now in ways he had not expected. He especially misses the shared humor.

Ralph also recalls when his father died suddenly from a heart attack and his mother mourned his absence for two years until one day she said, "I feel like myself again." Ralph shares that feeling.

He says he doesn't fear death. He had always heard you could die at any minute—get run over by a herd of elephants, fall of a cliff, etc. But now, getting closer to "the end," the fact that it is inevitable becomes more real. He remembers the first death in his family when he was about six years old and someone told him, "It's just like being asleep." That was scary to him instead of comforting. He was crying at night, afraid to go to sleep, wondering, "If I never wake up, where will I be?" He still wonders, pondering God and the universe and the mystery and majesty and unknowingness of it all. But in the meantime he enjoys the humor he sees everywhere, even when thinking he is either fourteen or fifty, floating, wondering, "What's next?"

Dear Lord, even though we rejoice and believe in your promise of eternal life, as the inevitability of death sinks in, we can't help but wonder what it will be like. Actually, we can't help but wonder what tomorrow or next week will be like! And I think maybe you made it that way, Lord, so we would never let the "wonder" seep out of our lives, so we could enjoy the humor and the friendship and the joy of each new day while we continue to think, "What's next?"

PRIME TIME

"The only time I think of myself as a senior citizen," says Sally Wilkes, "is when I find a good senior discount coupon!" Preferring to think of herself as a prime-timer, seventy-seven-year-old Sally still has a full-time career working for a large multi-national corporation.

When her supervisor told her they hoped she would never retire, Sally answered, "I have three criteria for staying: if my health continues to be good; if I continue to enjoy my job; and if the company continues to be satisfied with my work. If any of those three things change, then I'll retire."

Sally staunchly proclaims, "I think the senior years give you freedom! You no longer have to worry constantly about finding 'success,' question what career path to take, or ponder what you will be 'when you grow up.' Age also gives you freedom from self: less tension, less worry about always saying the right thing or making the right impression—and more self-assurance."

A Sally rule to live by is "never shut doors." As an example, she tells about a recent company picnic. "After lunch, they had lots of silly games. I could have skipped them, thinking I was too old for such foolishness but I tried every game, had a ball, and even won some prizes. And age was a benefit there too because wherever there was a line waiting to play, they insisted I go to the front of the line—and I did!"

Sally is disappointed that some of her friends feel they are too old to learn anything new. They shun the computer when she thinks they could be having lots of fun with the Internet.

Then she mentions another happy surprise that age had in store for her. She reports with a sly grin. "Now everybody's always hugging me. I guess it's become fashionable to hug seniors."

Life has not been all rosy for Sally, who had breast cancer a few years ago, has few surviving relatives, and lost her beloved husband of fifty-two years recently after a long illness. In spite of all that, Sally still feels these senior years are a prime time.

In addition to her career, she is very involved with activities at her church, belongs to several clubs, and enjoys travel. In the wintertime Sally even goes out some mornings when there's been a light snow and shovels her walk before leaving for work. Her neighbors get upset, thinking she shouldn't do that, but she says, "I like to do it because I'm just so grateful I still *can* do it."

Dear Lord, I know you've got to have courage to "never shut doors" but a closed-door policy can keep you from missing out on some opportunities or some fun like Sally's picnic games. On the other hand, Lord, I know it's also necessary to shut doors on troublesome memories of the past because dwelling on them takes up too much valuable time—time that could be spent on checking out any new doors that appear in the present. Dear Lord, please teach all of us past-fifty-folk to welcome new doors and know when to close old ones. Balancing the two could sure help us appreciate and enjoy being "prime-timers"!

You have to have other interests in life besides your own face, your own past. I try to see aging as a privilege. Aging allows me to do anything I want. It gives me freedom to speak up and tell the truth. JEANNE MOREAU

*I*t's young people who usually brag about being "free to be me," so who knew that age could be the place to find freedom! Now's the time to use your privilege to be a bit indulgent. If you want to have sausages and sauerkraut for breakfast, why not! If you want to read 'til 2 AM or eat crackers in bed, why not! Of course you might be prudent enough to not go skateboarding too often (except in your imagination!).

Maybe in earlier years, you were too busy for much meditation or spiritual study. Why not now? God has plenty of time so why not spend some of yours with him! Don't be afraid to talk about things you've never faced before, to delve deeper into that secret garden of spirituality. And don't just talk *at* God; invite God to talk back. You might be surprised at what he has to say. When you are forced to draw away from some of the more active parts of your life, draw closer to the inner you, where no one else can intrude, where there is only room for you and God to walk—or skip or jump or skateboard—together.

TAP DANCING
INTO RETIREMENT

Trixie had an exciting career working for a major advertising company in New York, riding the subways, hailing taxis, living in Gramercy Park, seeing Broadway shows, and loving the hurry-hurry of each day. When she retired, she moved to Williamsburg, Virginia, which is charming but has the relaxed ambiance of small-town America. She was afraid she would be bored by this lifestyle change, so naturally the first retirement activity she tried was tap dancing!

She heard of a retired classical ballerina who had opened a dance school and offered tap classes. Trixie joined a group of older dancing women who called themselves the "Step Sisters." They had fancy costumes and fancy routines and appeared at any local event that was looking for free entertainment. They were regulars at the local women's club luncheons and were on the program of the dance school's recitals, along with dance classes of all ages (including some young ballerinas who later made it into New

York ballet companies). One night they were invited to entertain at a club's dinner event at a hotel. Unfortunately, the hotel had marble floors—not great for tapping. When they consulted the management, workers kindly put down a *carpet* in the dance area—so their tapping turned into a soft-shoe act!

After a few years, Trixie tapped her way to a trick knee and was practical enough to give up dancing for other pursuits. She, who had been afraid of boredom, soon discovered she had something scheduled to do every day of the week—and thought she might have to downsize! Her favorite "job" now is that of a part-time classroom volunteer assistant to a Head Start Program teacher. She spends the day tying shoes, wiping noses, doing projects, going on field trips with a very active group of three-four-five year-olds—and she loves it. She says being with the kids really keeps you young.

The children come from "income challenged" families who are very supportive and bring cupcakes and other treats for birthdays. Trixie helps with testing the children before they enter the program and again later and says they are very responsive and *do* learn. Since she has always been a strong supporter of education, Trixie finds this a perfect retirement activity for her.

But she also finds time to sing in the church choir, go to concerts, lectures, and plays, and attend Lifelong Learning classes. This program offers three- to six-week classes on a variety of subjects, taught by retired college professors and CEOs from major companies—so it is a very stimulating way to "widen your world of knowledge." And to stir a bit of peaceful serenity in with kids, singing, studying, and having fun, Trixie has recently decided to take up yoga! She says that with this mix of anti-aging activities, she hopes to be like the kids and give a "head start" to her senior life.

Dear Lord, the old stereotype of aging certainly does not fit the many seniors who have found the way to not only lead a busy, happy life but also a useful one. Not all seniors can manage that, Lord, but for those who are doing it, like Trixie—it's quite a trick!

INVENTING
A LIFE

I've met a lot of inventive people but never knew anyone who invented something and actually got a patent in his name *until* I met Karl Sanderson. He has forty-one U.S. patents in his name and over one hundred patents in foreign countries like England, Japan, and Argentina.

Karl was born on his grandfather's homestead in Kansas, grew up on a farm, and never even dreamed of the places God planned to send him. He graduated from high school with top honors just when all the GIs were returning from WWII with the G.I. Bill to help them get a college education. After two years of crowded classes, Karl decided to join the Army himself so he too could get a G.I. Bill education.

The Army sent him to Europe where he had many "adventures" while serving as an English/German translator, visited Paris, the Riviera, Monaco, and "the sights" far away from Kansas. Although he had signed up for three years, the Korean War began and all enlistments were extended. Then, during a routine physical, the doctor discovered Karl only had sight in one eye and should never have been accepted in the Army! Now Karl was free to leave the Army but he stayed "where he was never supposed to be" and cashed in on that G.I. Bill.

Thanks to his student work with a professor, he was accepted in graduate school, got a PhD in chemistry from the University of Michigan, and then a position with a major chemical company. That's where he "invented" many new chemical compounds and began getting patents and making lots of money for his company. His work led to more travel including six weeks in Japan where he tried all the exotic foods including the startling "Dancing Shrimp" and the dangerous blowfish.

During this time, he also married the love of his life and they had seven children. He coached the kids' soccer and baseball teams, was a church usher (while his wife sang in the choir), was a member of a bowling team, a poker group, and a bridge group—and attended lots of Kansas reunions.

Even after retirement Karl continued as a consultant for the chemical company and then did a bit of teaching. One of his married daughters was then teaching high school chemistry and biology and she asked him to fill in and teach her class when she took maternity leave. The next school year, the principal called to invite him to come back part-time to teach chemistry and physical science—so he did that for another five years.

Now full retirement has given him time to watch the History Channel, read the kind of books that are heavy-lifting and heavy-reading, and spend lots of time with his ever-growing family and friends. He has never lost his interest in chemistry, and he and his son and a friend put together an amazing booklet that includes chemical reactions to outline a pattern of how the universe is organized. Karl says that is the first question he plans to ask God, "Is that the way the universe is organized? Did we get it right?"

Dear Lord, I can't even get my pantry organized so when I spoke to Karl, the translator, I could have used a translator myself when he started talking about chemistry and the universe. But, Lord, we certainly spoke the same language when he talked about his family, his faith, and his many interests and accomplishments. Thank you, Lord, for plucking people out of their comfort zone—like a Kansas farm—and sending them across the planet to teach and to invent new useful products and new faith-filled families.

THE SANDWICH GENERATION

Usually a happy-go-lucky person, Elsie Williams is an unmarried professional woman ruefully facing the challenges of retirement just when she has also discovered her very active but aging mother now needs extra care. She says she has new empathy for the "sandwich generation" of families who are still struggling to handle their own and their children's problems when they are also confronted with those of aging parents.

Elsie says, "The process of aging has been an adventure for me since the day I looked in the mirror and this gray-haired lady looked back and I said, 'Who are *you*?' For years, I had been telling myself, 'When I grow up, I'm going to be…' and suddenly I had to say to myself, 'You are.'

"It was a shock but I also saw it as a continuing adventure. Then I looked at the calendar and realized it was time to consider retiring. I was an executive, a bureaucrat who was always supposed to have the right answer, a person who was often interviewed by the media on the problem of the day and was expected to come up with an intelligent, reasoned response. My job gave me the respect of, and a value to, the community. Now, after thirty-four years, I was going to give that up. I began to worry, 'Who will I be when I give up this crutch?'

"When someone asked me, 'Why are you going to retire?' I responded, 'Because I can.' When someone else asked, 'What are you going to *do*?' I answered, '*Do*? I've been doing for years; now I'm going to discover me, find out who I am.'"

She now had time to read, garden, enroll in continuing education classes, and volunteer for various clubs. She was busy but she also wanted to rest and renew so she spent time journaling and seeking. And just then, she found herself in the unexpected role of caregiver. Her mother had always led an "involved" life but now she was suddenly not well, traveling with an oxygen tank and suffering from various setbacks. Elsie looked at her mother and thought, "When did *she* get old?" Elsie was not ready for the role reversal of taking care of her mother when her mother had always taken care of her.

After a brief period of "readjustment," Elsie is still basically her happy-go-lucky self as she continues her journaling, her discovery of self, and her questioning, "Who am I?" And she says, "In spite of everything, I consider this a wonderful time of life. I have a pension so I get paid to stay at home! What a deal! That gives me free time to care for my mother and we still have some good times together. So every day is still an adventure—and a blessing."

Dear Lord, most children realize there may come a day when they will need to help care for a parent—and they will want to do that—but sometimes it comes sooner than expected. Please help those adult children who may feel "sandwiched" to have the strength to be pulled from all sides without being pulled apart. It's a tall order and they may need a lot of help so, Lord, please watch over them and give them the kind of help only you can give. Please guide them and show them how being needed can be an opportunity to draw closer to a parent and maybe that will help them make this sandwich time a bit easier—and maybe even delicious.

A GUY'S LOOK
AT AGE

When George Reynolds was asked what he thought about aging, he quickly replied, "It's the best time of a guy's life!"

Since George has some physical problems and is moving rather slowly at eighty-five, I asked, "Why do you say that George?" He smiled and said, "Because by then you've lived long enough to finally knock some sense into your head."

Actually, George has made a lot of sense most of his life. An early childhood event left him with a bum leg but that didn't stop him for a minute. After high school, he got an office job so he could earn money for college and then left his family to move to the college town that he thought fit him best. He's been there ever since.

George tried a few jobs until he found one that would give him the opportunity to get promoted to a good position and good salary. He married, had children, and learned to play poker. For a number of years, he shuffled the cards and swapped jokes with a group of buddies who played once a month. They were really big spenders—they had a rule that you could never lose more than ten dollars! If you did, you just kept playing until you earned back some bucks.

Football was George's favorite for TV watching, especially Notre Dame football. So about thirty years ago he invited a bunch of guys to come over and watch the games on New Year's Day. His wife cooked up a big pot of bean soup and a big pan of cornbread. Some of the same guys are still coming every year—now bringing along some of their kids or grandkids. Bean Soup Day has become a tradition!

When George was working, no matter how icy or threatening the weather, he left the house extra early in the morning, treading carefully on his bum leg so he could be one of the first to get to the office. After he was safely at his desk, he allowed himself a second cup of coffee and looked over the newspaper. Today, after all those years of "dawn" rising, he relishes the chance to stay up late reading or having a midnight snack, and then he can sleep late into the day since he no longer has to hit the highway. After he reluctantly quit driving and sold his car, he's been content to stay snug at home with his books and his computer and visiting with friends who drop in.

There's a short list of places he still insists on going (maybe because he has to put up with his wife's driving!) He absolutely will *not* miss Mass on Sunday. He keeps an eye on the calendar so he will never miss time for a monthly haircut at his old barber's shop. And he enjoys an occasional stop at an I-Hop where he will pour about a gallon of syrup on an unsuspecting Belgian waffle.

His simple lifestyle might not suit someone else but to George, it's the best time of a guy's life.

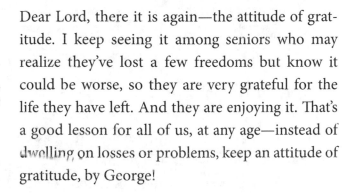

Dear Lord, there it is again—the attitude of gratitude. I keep seeing it among seniors who may realize they've lost a few freedoms but know it could be worse, so they are very grateful for the life they have left. And they are enjoying it. That's a good lesson for all of us, at any age—instead of dwelling on losses or problems, keep an attitude of gratitude, by George!

I like living. I have sometimes been wildly, despairingly, acutely miserable, racked with sorrow, but through it all I still know that quite certainly just to be alive is a grand thing.   AGATHA CHRISTIE

I seem to remember that this is the same Agatha Christie who once said, "My husband is an archaeologist, so the older I get, the better he likes me." She obviously could laugh at herself and had a positive attitude about aging. True, the limitations of aging can make it all too easy to be despairing, miserable, racked with regrets—but letting such feelings rule the day just adds to life's limitations. Instead, many of today's seniors wake up every day and say, "Thank you, Lord, for another day." Then they try to make the most of each new day, whatever it is, drinking in the blessings and seeing problems as an opportunity to understand and share in the sorrows of others. They have the attitude that makes it possible to agree that "just to be alive is a grand thing!"

THE FRENCH CONNECTION

L ily wears her hair pulled straight back into a French knot, which clears the way for you to see all of her smiling face. When she smiles, her whole face lights up in delight and her eyes actually twinkle. And she is such a happy, pleasant person, she smiles a lot—especially when she starts telling you about her French connection.

Around the time of World War I, her father traveled from France to America and fell in love with a Southern belle. He was sent here on business because he had attended an English school and spoke English better than others in his company. When he returned to France, he took along the Memphis belle as his bride. His business prospered and his family grew until the brink of World War II. By then there had been many family trips back and forth between France and America and, fearing what was to come, her father decided it was time for his wife and children to journey to Memphis to be safe with their American relatives.

When Hitler began advancing in Europe, her father decided it was time for him too to head for Memphis and he was able to get passage on the last American ship sailing to New York. Halfway across, they were stopped by a German ship and all the passengers were told to get into lifeboats before they sank the ship. But at the last minute, the ship's captain received a message from Hitler. According to Lily's family story, Hitler said something like, "Don't sink the ship. I want to finish with Europe before I take on America." Her father was able to reboard and the ship arrived safely.

Now the French connection takes a reverse turn. Lily was twenty years old, with those twinkling eyes and a charming French accent, when she came to live in America and she soon met a young Southern doctor who fell in love with her. Six weeks after they met, they were married and history repeated itself—this time with a French bride and a Southern groom.

Lily surprised her husband when he discovered she knew *nothing* about cooking but she soon learned and eventually even won a couple of cooking contests. She also did a lot of cooking to feed their seven children—five boys and two girls. She said people were always telling her, "I took French in high school but I love to hear you talk and I wish I had studied it more." So Lily founded the Alliance Française, a school where people could learn about the language and all things French. When asked if she herself taught there, Lily said, "How could I with those seven children?"

She said she was shy but blossomed in America. She was also always a happy person and still radiates happiness with those twinkling eyes. She says, "Why waste time being miserable when, wherever you look, you can find joy?"

Lily was in her eighties when she moved into an assisted living home and she loves it. She says the workers are such sweet people and she has made some delightful new friends. She has always loved classical music and a gentleman who sits at the same dining table shares her interest and "escorts" her to a symphony concert held every Friday night in their building. When asked, "Does this mean you have a gentleman friend," she flashes that lovely smile and says, "Well…yes."

Her five sons all followed in their grandfather's steps and have careers in insurance. Their business cards have a picture of the grandparents—the proper French businessman and the Memphis belle wearing a huge flower-bedecked hat. And just recently, one of the sons won a trip to France. He immediately bought two more tickets, one for his mother and one for his sister to accompany her. So, now nearing ninety, Lily is off to visit France where she will see her brother, who still lives in the family home where she grew up. Lily, of the great smile and twinkling eyes, will be coming home.

Dear Lord, what a wonderful experience to meet someone who, after moving to a new country, raising seven children, and being a widow for twenty-four years, still sees joy wherever she looks. Somehow, Lord, I can see your reflection in those twinkling eyes. Thank you for giving me that opportunity.

CLEANLINESS
IS NEXT TO...

As a young girl, Willie Mae came from the South to a large Midwestern town where she happily worked in the food service area of a university *until* she was in a serious automobile accident. By the time she recovered from her injuries, her job there was gone so she "switched careers" and became the best cleaning lady in town.

She was a real professional—cleaning in, around, under, behind and in every nook and cranny. And her hard work and never-ending cheeriness soon made her a "member of the family" wherever she went. One of her "clients" was in a wheelchair so, in addition to cleaning, Willie Mae became her aide, driving her places and helping her shop, and other activities. When this lady died, Willie Mae continued cleaning for the lady's daughters. And that's how it was with all her clients. Whenever anyone's situation changed and they couldn't have Willie Mae work for them anymore, they recommended her to a friend.

Her calendar was always full, regularly scheduled at various homes five days a week. She saw to it that all her employers reported her earnings and paid Social Security for her so when Willie Mae got to the age to be eligible for benefits, she retired from cleaning and drew her pension.

In the meantime, Willie Mae had married and had a daughter and later a grandson and was very involved with her church and her extended family. She took care of her aging mother until it was necessary to move her into a nursing home. By then, Willie Mae had retired, so her days were free and she visited her mother every day for a year and a half until her mother died at the age of ninety-two. In addition to her mother, Willie Mae also cheered up the other ladies at the home and regularly took them little gifts or made a cake for them to share or played the piano so they could have sing-alongs. After her mother's death, Willie Mae has continued to be a regular, welcomed visitor to the nursing home.

By being in contact with so many older people, Willie Mae sees what a difference "attitude" makes in a person's life. She sees how some who have terrible problems still enjoy life and make the most of whatever time they have left while others, with less trouble, dwell on the negatives and miss out on the joy.

Today, at age seventy-three, Willie Mae has extended her cheer-up visits to several nursing homes, volunteers at the Salvation Army, cares for her eighty-two-year-old husband, and plays the piano for funerals at two funeral homes as well as at her church.

She says, "An idle mind is the devil's workshop so I keep busy." She admits that there are a few days when she has to stop for a nap or take things a bit slower than before but, deep down, she doesn't feel any different than she ever did.

As a Missionary Minister at the church where her brother is the pastor, her work has brought in many new members. She and other helpers make up Easter baskets and Christmas stockings for about two hundred children at the church every year.

Willie Mae says she never watches television. Instead she spends her evenings reading the Bible and making "phone visits" to people who have asked for prayers or who live alone or need a bit of cheer.

When asked how she feels about getting older, Willie Mae quickly replies, "I'm just too busy to think about it."

Dear Lord, many seventy-somethings like Willie Mae spend their retirement years by helping others. They find many little thoughtful ways to bring cheer into others' lives—even if it's a phone visit or a shared prayer or a good laugh. It's like a "ministry" for them to spread God's love around in everyday ways. And, like Willie Mae, they are just too busy being useful to have time to worry about getting "old."

HELP WANTED!
A CARETAKER FOUND!

When I get together with my young friend, Millie Sanders, we talk about books and children and aging. That's because she's a reader, a mother, and a certified recreational therapist who works primarily with seniors who live in assisted living or in nursing homes. When I asked why she had chosen aging as her specialty, she replied, "I didn't choose it. It chose me." Millie explained that she had started out with plans to do rehab—but to focus on pediatrics. While getting her degree, she worked with various ages and discovered that she felt "called" to work with seniors instead of children.

Since those residing in assisted living may be a lively group, Millie arranges a variety of activities for them— music, painting, crafts, bus trips to tour local places of interest or just to visit an ice cream shop. She tries to learn their individual interests and plan programs around them. She says what many of them want is just to talk to someone who will listen.

Millie says, "I like to listen to them. Their stories matter—to them and to me. I feel fortunate that I am the one to be their listener. And by learning about them, I know what kind of activities to arrange to keep their life interesting. One lady told me she had always wanted to learn how to paint on china, so I was able to borrow some equipment from another facility and we had a china painting class. One man said he liked to play cards so I got together a group who joined him for regular card games."

Millie also invites speakers, lecturers, and musical groups to present programs. Once she knows individual interests, she tries to form a circle of friends who might like to knit together, form a book discussion club, a Bible study or prayer group, or even a wood-working or repair group for men (whom she might also recruit to help with small repairs in the building). In addition, she encourages individual activities like working crossword puzzles, playing computer games, and writing notes to friends. She is always looking for something new, a different way to stimulate the brain and creativity—or, as she puts it, "to create small moments of joy."

In addition to assisted living homes, Millie has worked at nursing homes where people were once over-medicated and left to just sit quietly as the days passed. Today she says they are often much happier places where even people with some dementia can be content. She says she is often tempted to tell children of such patients to "forget the quiz!" Asking questions like, "Do you know what day it is? Do you know who I am?" may be frightening and frustrating for the person who is trying to remember but just can't. Instead she suggests you "embrace them wherever they are instead of expecting them to come into *your* reality." As a therapist for such patients, she again sees herself as a listener, calmly relieving distress by listening to their stories and thoughts, validating them instead of scolding—reminiscing even if they tell the same story or ask the same question over and over.

Obviously, this is not an easy job but Millie sees it as a ministry and a creative way to help people who need help even though they may not remember who you are or how you helped them. She says, at a time when many people hate their jobs, she feels blessed because she really loves her work.

Dear Lord, it's very hard to deal with the loss of a relative or friend through death but it might be even worse to watch someone you love disappear due to the cruel loss of memory. They are still present but you have lost their presence. Yet they still need our visits, and our hugs might comfort them if only for a little while.

My friend Jack told me that he regularly visits his father-in-law who was a vibrant, savvy business man and a great husband and father before he developed Alzheimer's. Jack said he starts every visit by saying the same thing, "Hi, Mr. Goodman. I'm Jack. I married your daughter." Mr. Goodman looks at him, smiles, and always says, "Well, congratulations." Somehow this triggers a memory and Mr. Goodman launches into a story. It may be a story Jack has heard many times before. But it might be a scandalous or humorous story about some local business deal from the past that is news to Jack—and of great interest! Either way, they both enjoy the visit—maybe because neither one knows what to expect! Lord, bless all the caring relatives and workers who treasure seniors "where they are" and thanks for that little bit of humor we often find in even sad situations.

YOU'VE GOT MAIL

Sister John Marie says, "I begin my day reading Scripture—and then I check my e-mail!" Nearing her ninetieth birthday, this Catholic nun still happily combines the spiritual world with the real one. When asked what she thinks of old age, she quickly responds, "I wouldn't have missed it for anything."

She explains, "When I was younger, there was only time to do. Now there's time to be. Before, exteriors were always breaking in on my interior life, my spiritual life. I wasn't listening, wasn't waiting to hear. Now I have time to listen, to pay attention, to seek and find new meanings."

Sister related how in her childhood, all the games and stories, joys and surprises of every day were anchored in the "ability" of her body—and scheduled time had no meaning. Even a serious childhood illness was not an interruption of life; it was part of the "now" of childhood. But as she grew older, time became a measuring tool. The clock and the calendar figured in her plans. Illness was a hindrance, a nuisance that stole the time she had planned for something else. Now that she is even older, her body has again become a deciding factor in her days.

Sister says, "If I wake in the morning feeling wonderful, I rejoice and know I am being given a day, or perhaps a half day, or it may be just a few hours during which I can pick up some of my past interests. I no longer watch the clock. When my energy runs low, I merely stop what I am about and spend the remainder of the day being delightfully lazy. Tomorrow—if there is a tomorrow—my day may last longer. It is as if *another* directs my life and all I am asked to do is to let it happen."

Sister recalls times in her childhood when, as she played alone with paper dolls or picture books, she was filled with a surge of awe and peace and inner joy. She now recognizes those experiences as moments of prayer when God spoke to her. Today she says, "I find myself feeling at home again with this simple type of praying, of letting myself be drawn into an awareness of God…and once again, time loses its importance. It's a beautiful time of life for me."

Of course, this does not mean that Sister spends all her time praying. No indeed. When she retired from teaching at sixty-five, she moved into a residence on a college campus where she had the opportunity to meet students, traveling professors, and lecturers from many states and countries, which gave her material for writing books and articles as a way of continuing to "teach" through her writing. Her published articles have covered subjects from Dolly Dingle paper dolls to bamboo to classroom ideas for teachers to deep spirituality. This second career led her to learn about computers and the e-mail she still uses to keep in touch with friends and former students.

She likes to explore the mysteries of the computer by pressing different buttons "just to find out what will happen." She has discovered how to make her own computer greeting cards. And she also makes candy to share with the other Sisters and to give as gifts for every occasion.

Sister has now moved into a lovely retirement home for nuns where she feels her greatest blessing is to be able to observe how the other Sisters there react to all the stages of old age so that she herself can learn from them. She says, "I would have missed so much if I had died sooner. Age is a natural part of life. If you fight against it too long, you spoil it. If you accept it, you are free to be yourself. Our human diminishment is the necessary change that we undergo to find a richer life…and time itself comes to naught since we are born for eternity."

Dear Lord, I guess Sister John Marie is a good example of how you're never too old to learn—even if it's learning about aging! She says she spends some time each day reading to the "older" Sisters so, as she nears ninety, her days are still filled with "serving" others plus prayer and allowing another to direct her life. Sounds like she's still teaching by example everyone she encounters. Thanks, Lord, for letting me be one of her lucky pupils.

I seldom think about my limitations, and they never make me feel sad. Perhaps there is just a touch of yearning at times, but it is vague, like a breeze among flowers. HELEN KELLER

*E*ach of us is given the same number of hours each day, yet we each choose to use them in such different ways. Some use the hours to concentrate on the negatives of life, and life becomes negative. Others look for new possibilities, and life becomes a blessing. At times when the touch of yearning insinuates itself, some dwell on it and turn it into a frightful storm. Others accept it as a breeze among flowers.

IT'S A MYSTERY!

Successful mystery writer Steve Cook says exercising your brain is probably even more important than exercising your body. When he left his long-time banking career, he did not see himself wearing the label of retirement. He saw this stage of life as the opportunity to go into a new career, the opportunity to do something he had always wanted to do but never had the time— the chance to become an author. He had always loved mystery and history and that's what he wanted to write about.

With time now at his disposal, Steve wasn't interested in playing tennis, traveling around the world, or hitting the senior circuit. He thought all these were worthy pursuits for others but he just wanted to read and write. He enrolled in writing classes, joined writers' groups, attended seminars, workshops, and conferences, and collected and read lots of reference books. Then he wrote and entered writing contests and collected rejection slips. After several years of honing his new craft and refusing to be discouraged by rejection, Steve found an agent who was interested in the idea for a series of books Steve had submitted. Finding an agent is a great achievement for any writer but there was more good news to come. The agent negotiated with a publisher and got Steve a contract to publish three books!

Steve's mystery/history books have taken him and his readers to exotic places to get involved with fascinating plots and interesting characters. As a result of their success, today Steve travels to mystery writers' conventions, teaches the kinds of classes he once attended, and is now working on his next novel. He loves his new career and has to keep a "to do" list to stay organized and keep up with all the adventures in his non-retiring years. He says he paces himself and believes in a healthy diet, a proper amount of sleep, and long walks on the beach. And he always saves time to visit and enjoy the company of his grandchildren. (As most grandparents know, there's no mystery about the fun of making history with the next generation!)

Dear Lord, it's not as easy as it looks to put words on paper and then wish and pray that someone will read them and be entertained or inspired by them. Steve could have given up after he received the first few rejection letters but he persevered. And that's one thing senior citizens have to learn—persever- ance. The slower your steps become, the faster the time goes and the more perseverance is required to get the simplest tasks done, all of which are easier than getting a book published! But he did it—and entertained and inspired a whole lot of folks, including his grandchildren! Thanks, Lord, for all the mystery of life and all the history-mak- ing seniors.

A MIND MAKES ITSELF

Today journaling—keeping a daily log of happenings and feelings—has become a popular activity for many but it isn't a new idea. A lot of people have kept diaries for brief times in their lives but I have heard about a woman who has kept a notebook from the time she was only eight years old! Mary Sue Smith was always writing down her own thoughts or reading books to discover others' thoughts and she always felt that some day she might write a book herself. Instead, after college, she tried such disparate jobs as being a model, then a clerk, and a social worker. Soon she married, had children, and immersed herself into a "woman's" life.

Somehow, after reading so much great literature, although she continued the notebook and wrote poems, she lacked the self-confidence to try to join the ranks of authors. Eventually, she became almost physically sick from the need to make herself heard. While enrolled in a writing course, some of her semi-autobiographical stories about a fictional family were published in a prestigious magazine. Her career was beginning. This was followed by her first book, which was a collection of short stories (possibly based on some of her journal notes) and then, at the age of fifty, her first novel was published.

Although she was a slow, painstaking writer, in the next forty years, she continued publishing novels, lecturing on literature, and teaching creative writing at several colleges. Some critics were mesmerized by her intellectually challenging fiction and complex plots. Some were intrigued by her "filigreed" sentences and the way she had of telling a story. And age did not slow her down. After getting that late start at the age of fifty, she continued turning out novels, two of which were published when she was in her eighties and one in her nineties.

In discussing her career she once said, "A mind is not given but makes itself, out of whatever is at hand and sticking tape—and it is not a private possession but an offering. I have always had to write everything, no matter the subject, as if my life depended upon it. Of course— it does."

Dear Lord, few people are blessed with enough energy to continue doing productive work after the age of ninety but thank you for the ones who are. Remind us that our lives are not "private possessions but an offering." Remind us to offer all to you every day in every way. And help us all, of any age, Lord, to be aware that minds should continue to be "exercised" as well as bodies, even if we have to use whatever is at hand and try to keep it all together with sticking tape.

IT'S IN THE BOOK

Everybody loved Marie Prentiss. She was everybody's favorite English teacher for many years. And Marie loved books. She *loved* to read. When she retired, she took a part-time job at a bookstore so she could be near books. She enjoyed retirement, making cookies with the grand-children, walking the dog, and having plenty of time to read. Fortunately, her husband loved books too, so they spent many happy hours cosily reading in their lovely home. And then Marie started a book discussion group at the bookstore where she worked.

She simply put a little note by the cash register inviting people to meet on a Wednesday at noon. A surprisingly varied group of people accepted the invitation, and Marie explained she would suggest a book to be read and they would simply meet once a month and share ideas about the meaning and message of the book. The group includ-ed mostly women plus a few brave men. Although they were of various ages and backgrounds, Marie's quiet introductions and handling soon merged them into a circle of friends. They sometimes had very different ideas about the books and the authors but no one ever got mad or upset. Instead, they enjoyed being surprised by the nuances that each suggested. And they all looked forward to the once-a-month Wednesday get-together and really hated to miss a single one.

After ten years or so, the group was still together when Marie's husband developed Alzheimer's and she mourned when he had to go to a nursing home. Not long after, Marie's hand began to tremble occasionally. She finally explained to the group that she had been diagnosed with Parkinson's Disease. She continued inspiring and "teaching" her group as long as she could. And then she had to ask them to keep the group together without her, which they did. They send her cards and call and keep in touch and vow to keep the group going in her honor. It is still a circle of friends but it isn't quite the same without the guidance and quiet presence of Marie.

She struggled as the doctors continued trying different medicines. But the worst side effect of the illness and the medicines was that Marie was no longer able to read. With help, she could go grocery shopping or occasionally out for a quiet lunch but she just could not read—the one thing she had enjoyed most of her life.

That's when her ingenious daughter began trying new ways to make her life bearable. She brought in tiny pots of herbs and they started an herb garden on the windowsill. She brought in a new puppy and they watched his antics as he grew. She bought jigsaw puzzles and put them on a table so that Marie's helpers could have something to do when Marie took the many naps that were now necessary. And sometimes Marie could help find the puzzle pieces. Next her daughter heard of a charity that needed people to make sandwiches that they could deliver to the homeless. Marie and her daughter began doing that. By now, Marie could do very little but she could still be useful and do something to help others.

All the while, her daughter has kept praying for Marie. She tried books on tape or reading to her mother but long stories were just too tiresome. Then she found a big book of short stories and, today, when Marie needs to rest, her daughter quietly reads those to her. And the book discussion group continues reading and discussing and missing her because everybody loves Marie.

Dear Lord, age has its joys and rewards but sometimes it comes with a high price tag—losing something you miss most. For Marie, it's reading; for others it may be driving, gardening, golfing, or fishing. Bless them all, Lord, and help them see the blessing of gentle caretakers and loving family and friends.

NEVER ON SUNDAY

"I work two days a week now to pay for my insurance—but never on Sunday or Wednesday. I gotta save those days for God and garage sales!" So says Barbara Reynolds who isn't old enough yet for Medicare but has had a lot of health problems that led her to a shorter work week—but also to new experiences. Barbara explains, "I've been a daughter, sister, wife, mother, and grandmother; now it's time to be Barbara."

After recovering from a bout of congestive heart failure that put her on life support for a bit, Barbara is aware of death and could feel negative or frightened by the future. Instead, she has a new, more relaxed attitude about life. Many things don't matter as much anymore. Material things are less important. She spends her time taking courses, getting together with her family, browsing those Wednesday garage sales, or going wherever the day leads because, "Now I can do whatever I want without asking anybody." She does, however, carry a cell phone just in case a grandchild calls to ask for a ride or a favor.

Barbara and her daughter have moved in together to cut expenses and to form a support system. Barbara says, "She has called 911 several times for me, and when she had an operation, I was there for her." On Mother's Day, her daughter gave her a card with the words, "To Mother, who would rather have roses on her table than diamonds around her neck." Barbara smiled and said, "I'm so glad she could recognize that about me."

She also mentions a son who told her, "Don't think about moving in with me. I'm not taking care of in-laws, outlaws, or anybody." Yet when Barbara was seriously ill, her son showed up and insisted on sleeping on the floor beside her bed "just in case Mom needs me."

Barbara grew up in the country, was married for seventeen years, raised three children, took care of her ailing mother, worked as a supervisor in a factory, then answered an ad in the paper and was hired and trained to be an optical assistant at a discount store. That's where she now spends those two days a week.

Barbara is very proud of her children because they are all "faithful Christians." She says, "They don't smoke or drink or use drugs. And they respect me. Who could be any richer?"

Dear Lord, being on life support and facing death can certainly get your attention—plus bring major changes and challenges to your lifestyle. But those changes and challenges just might lead you to appreciate and even enjoy life more. When we face major or even minor changes in our lifestyles, Lord, help us be as brave and positive as Barbara and turn those groans into grins.

'Twixt the optimist and pessimist,
the difference is droll;
The optimist sees the doughnut,
But the pessimist sees the hole.

MCLANDBURGH WILSON

*H*ealth problems are a major concern of anyone who is a senior or an almost-senior. They can change a lifestyle in an instant, and they can become the focus of everyday life. But they can also be an opportunity to let go of some of the "duties" that seemed so all-important, the acquisitions that seemed so necessary, the little details that took up so much time. Of course, this is not a minor adjustment. It is not an easy task. It is not something to take lightly. Or maybe it is. Maybe taking it lightly is one way to still be in control. You can choose to dwell on the misery or you can try to see the little chuckles in mistakes made, try to rejoice in each small victory toward recovery, try to accept this as a time to look inside and find out who you are or who you want to be. It's a challenge but it's more fun to enjoy the doughnut instead of worrying about what's missing in the middle.

THE GREATEST CONSOLATION

What does a retired newspaperman do in his "old age"? Why, he becomes the star of a popular local TV show, of course! And where does he get his energy and inspiration? Well, he has two resources. One is his busy get-up-and-go wife who keeps him on schedule, and the other is a life-long habit of daily Mass, which he says is the "greatest consolation."

Roger laughs and says, "I never ever thought about getting old when I was in my sixties and seventies but now that I've passed that eighty mark I occasionally think I might like to put my feet up and rest a while—but my wife won't let me. She is so vital, I draw strength from her positive attitude." Roger and his wife, Flora, have always been active in their parish but their interests reach far and wide, both locally and nationally.

Roger's career included various journalism jobs including editorial page editor of a large Midwest metropolitan newspaper. He served as president of many community organizations, including the Backstoppers (a group that supports families of police officers and firefighters who have lost their lives in the line of duty). Then Roger retired and became a TV star! As the host of a PBS talk-show that features area radio and TV personalities discussing hot topics in the news of the day every week, Roger has added to his reputation as a local celebrity.

And Flora, not to be outdone by her husband, has done volunteer work, won lots of awards, been to the White House to shake hands with President Reagan, and continues to be very active in a national organization which she helped found. She recalls how this important organization began with a few people meeting in her living room when her five children were still young. She says, "It isn't easy trying to change the world from your living room but after all these years, we're still working on it."

During a recent visit to their home, the phones kept ringing and it was a beehive of activity, with a fax coming in for Flora that had to be answered immediately, an urgent phone call for Roger, and another appointment scheduled for the next hour.

At the parish, they've both been leaders for many years in Journey to Faith, an instructive program for converts or returning Catholics. Roger is a communion minister at a local hospital one day a week and also takes communion to homebound parishioners. Flora is busy with many church and civic activities and keeps tabs on their children, grandchildren, and great-grandchildren.

Roger says, "We're blessed to have good health and time now to visit with friends and family. Through the TV show, we meet people of all ages and feel that we benefit by meeting younger ones as well as those who are over fifty. When I was an editor, every day there was a fresh page, something new happening—just like life with Flora! Someone once said to me, 'Your wife is outspoken,' and I laughingly replied, 'By whom?'"

This octogenarian couple is grateful and happy to be able to continue their busy lifestyle, although they do admit to having to slow down just a bit. Roger says, "We couldn't keep going without the spiritual refreshment of our faith, daily Mass—and my 'outspoken,' energetic wife."

Dear Lord, most people who leave full-time employment don't get the chance for a TV career but plenty of today's seniors sure do keep on the go, dashing from one new pursuit to another—and they love it. However, adding years does not usually add energy, so some seniors (like maybe me?) may have to take the ecologists' advice to "conserve energy" in more ways than one. Lord, help us learn from wise seniors like Roger and Flora who know that "slow down" may be an aggravation but not a stop sign. Even when it's necessary to cut out a few "trivial pursuits," keeping on the go can help you still keep going and trying to "change the world," even if it's only your small slice of it.

DEAR DIARY

"*28 December 1944*. After arriving in Boas, we were told the town and the German Red Cross had been bombed so there was no food for us."

"*29 December 1944*. We were marched to a railroad siding and mounted in boxcars. Fifty-two men in our car so we were pretty crowded and it looked like no sleep in sight. After eleven days of marching and going a distance of 250 kilometers we were happy though to get any sort of ride."

"*30 December 1944*. Really had a trip by rail… five days with no food, water only twice…what a mess we were when we finally arrived at New Brandenburg."

These quotes do not come from the kind of diary you might expect but it is very dear to those who have inherited it from a WWII survivor of a prisoner of war camp.

It relates a story that could come from many American GIs in WWII but it was recorded in a wartime log by a twenty-seven-year-old we'll call Captain Paul, who was a member of an armored division near Bastogne when they "ran into at least a full Panzer division." Outmanned and outgunned, many were killed or wounded and some, like Paul, were captured.

The amazing thing about the diary or log is that Paul never complained or whined about his miserable situation. He just recorded what was happening. He was always positive, sometimes humorous, recording a bit of joking with a German guard or being "surprised" by "potato soup again!"

One entry is an indication of his amazing spirit:

> "*24 December 1944.* For supper tonight we had one-fourth of a beet and a cup of hot water. Mine didn't stay down so I don't think I'll try that menu again....Had a very nice Christmas service conducted by Father Sampson, who is the Catholic chaplain we picked up at the last town. Never—as long as I live—will I ever forget that service. It was wonderful under the circumstances."

Years later, when his son asked him what kept him going as a POW, the Captain simply said, "You learn to pray a lot."

More years later, when the Captain died, several of his fellow POWs came to the funeral and one told Paul's son, "Your dad saved my life. It was his positive, hopeful, cheerful encouragement that kept me going when I was ready to give up."

Today there are many WWII veterans who are in their eighties or nineties and are still positive, hopeful, cheerful examples of the American spirit. One more quote from Paul's "diary" pertains to that.

> *"9 January 1945.* ...got sick and was taken to the dispensary...had lost almost forty pounds since being captured. The men in the hospital (Americans) really treated me royally...It made me realize what a wonderful thing an honest-to-God American G.I. is."

Dear Lord, thanks for all the brave soldiers who have fought for their country and have helped the lives of others. Even though there are often unpleasant difficulties in the "later" years, Lord, remind seniors that you can always find something cheerful, hopeful, positive, or maybe even humorous—if you look hard enough for it—just like Paul did in his "diary." And, Lord, I'm sure you would agree we should all take Paul's advice when he simply said, "You learn to pray a lot."

BOOKS, PAINTINGS, AND A HOUSEBOAT

When I watch *Jeopardy* on TV, I know enough about a little to compete until they come to famous authors. Now this should be a good category for a non-famous author but I keep getting their names mixed up. But since we are not using real names in this book anyway, I'll tell you about a famous author we will call William Whaley. It was of interest to me that he didn't get his first book published until he was fifty-three years old—three years beyond AARP's definition of a senior! Actually, he had been shopping the book about for a long time but when it finally did get published, it won the National Book Award for best first novel and was a finalist for the Pulitzer Prize for fiction!

Until then, he had considered himself primarily an artist but this success encouraged him to write a dozen more books, three of which became Hollywood movies. Then he said, "Not thinking of myself as a writer gives me the freedom to be one."

On the way to getting published, Whaley served in WWII and resolved to some day return to Europe to paint. After he earned a degree in art and a doctorate in psychology, he did move his family to Paris—where they lived on a houseboat! While his wife taught kindergarten, he painted in the streets and often invited passers-by who admired his art to come home to dinner, hoping they might buy a painting. Money was often short but he persisted in both painting and writing—before and after he was fifty-three years old.

When one of his daughters was considering marriage, she called to ask him "What is love?" Since Dad was paying for the long-distance call and money was still scarce then, he evidently decided to keep it short. She says he told her, "As far as I can tell, it is passion, admiration, and respect. If you have two, you have enough. If you have all three, you don't have to die to go to heaven."

Whaley lived the life many people only dream about. It probably wasn't all as "heavenly" as it may sound but he didn't give up chasing his dream when he was past fifty and "too old" to keep trying. As a result, his persistence and his passion for the art of life finally earned him success, admiration, and respect.

Dear Lord, chasing dreams might be easier for the young and fleet of foot but a lot of seniors have had dreams come true in their later years. Most don't dream of going to Paris to live on a houseboat but many have achieved different kinds of dreams—either great or small. Some have started a new part-time career or found a new hobby. Some have traveled somewhere for fun—either across the world or just across town. Some have found new friends by volunteering or joining some kind of study group or social club. Even though elder dreams may take a little extra effort and a lot of extra prayer, it's never too late to try something new. Lord, thank you for so many possibilities in today's "senior" world.

A man is not old until regrets take the place of dreams.   JOHN BARRYMORE

*D*reaming does not belong exclusively to the young. It's one thing that is still affordable, can be done in any place in any kind of weather, and is not fattening. Of course, some dreams require action, work, and stick-to-it-iveness—like competing in the Senior Olympics or starting a second career. But some dreams require only an easy chair where you can cast aside regrets and rejoice in all the ways you have made the most of life—the ways you have helped others, the family gatherings, the trips, the time you rode a merry-go-round or a bicycle or went to the top of the Empire State Building. Other dreams help you look toward the future where you will think of ways you can still help others, where you will plan to surprise someone with a gift or a letter, where you will say a prayer for someone who needs one, where you will make a list of all the things you can still do (with or without help), and where you will say a great big prayer of thanksgiving for all the blessings that still fill your days. And that's a way to dream yourself younger!

HAVE WEAPON,
WILL TRAVEL

When she was a very young girl planning to enter the convent, Sister Mary Carol recalls receiving a list of all the things she was expected to bring with her to the motherhouse. Included on the list was a pocket knife. Sister says, "I can still remember thinking, 'I didn't know nuns carried knives!'"

But indeed she did carry that pocket knife in her many travels, teaching in a variety of midwestern schools. She explains how it had so many uses at school, opening boxes or cellophane packets, turning stubborn screws, or cutting the string on an errant kite. And today when she lives in a convalescent home for nuns, Sister still keeps her trusty pocket knife in her pocket. She says, "I've gone through several little knives in my ninety-one years but I still like to have one with me to open an envelope or repair something."

Sister has always been good at repairing things and "making do" at all the small-town schoolhouses where she has taught. One was so close to a railroad, the schoolroom literally shook each time a train rumbled by. She still recalls many of the children's names and tells how she converted packing boxes into file cabinets, and a chocolate-covered-cherry candy box into an index-card holder.

Now that she is slightly limited by a recent stroke, she says she watches the nurses moving quickly about, doing the kind of chores she can no longer manage, and she sometimes feels that she has lost the person she used to be. Her humor, her insight, her personality are all still there but she realizes that now it is time to be a slightly different person—to accept instead of always giving.

Sister is grateful for the blessings of the place where she lives now—the delicious food, the entertainments, the prayer gatherings with other Sisters, and the loving care she receives from the nurses. She says, "I don't deserve it but I drink it in."

And to "exercise the brain" and have some fun, she and some of the other nuns have formed a poetry club. To give it focus, at the end of each meeting they select a word or a phrase and before the next meeting, they each write a poem or a free verse centered on that thought. When they share their work, it's amazing and refreshing to see how many different ideas can come from the same topic.

So Sister is not mourning her former self. She laughingly says, "I always thought when I got old, I would just spend all day praying, but there's too much going on here for that. Instead, I keep saying short prayers of hope and love and offer up my limitations. I know there are bits of my former self missing now but this is my opportunity to share in the cross and the suffering of others. And I rejoice that I have so few problems. Some of my former self is still alive and well. And I am still a nun who carries a knife!"

Dear Lord, I was certainly surprised that nuns were expected to have a pocket knife, but it sounds like that could really come in handy for a teacher. Maybe I should carry an imaginary pocket knife so I could cut short that snappy comeback I threaten to hurl at my husband or cut out a few of those "rest" periods when I could turn off the TV and use the time to hurl a few prayers your way. Help me, Lord, to follow Sister's example, to offer up limitations while rejoicing in the parts of my former self that are still alive and kicking. Or, come to think of it, maybe I could also cut out some of that kicking!

IN THE NEWS

I keep finding more stories in the news about people who have passed the ninety-year mark and even beyond! I saw a newspaper story about a woman who had published her memoirs when she was in her eighties and nineties. She told of rural France during World War I and the bizarre turn of events that kept her trapped in Germany during WWII. She wrote of fears and shadows but also of comic moments. In her youth, she studied at the Sorbonne, and worked as a school teacher and as an actress in Italian films. She married a fervent anti-Nazi German painter, but when they returned to Germany for a short visit, he was called up for military service and she was left to fend for herself.

She scraped together a living with such jobs as a weaver in a fishing village and as a translator. When she was hired to translate German mystery books, she transformed the tall, blonde handsome heroes into squat dark-haired men with fleshy noses! Near the end of the war she lived in a house alone in the Black Forest and helped escaped Polish prisoners of war get to the Swiss border. After the war, she and her husband emigrated to the United States and she wrote children's books, which he illustrated.

Nearing the century mark, she was still at work, writing short stories about her early experiences in New York. She was quoted as saying, "I'm often not happy when my writing does not go the way I want" but she kept at it—a survivor who lived a life of ordeals and opportunities and spiced it all with a tart sense of humor.

Then I read about a lady who, at ninety, is still telling people where to get off! She works every Saturday and on holidays, greeting motorists at a state visitors' center where she hands out maps and tells motorists how to get where they're hoping to go or where to find a place to stay or to get a good meal. She says, "I sure know how to give directions."

And there was the story of a couple who had been married for eighty years! She was ninety-eight and he was one-hundred-one. She had some health problems but he appeared to be in excellent health, still had good eyesight, and could walk without any kind of aids.

The article quoted him as saying he was amazed he had lived so long especially since he had had some close calls in his youth. He said he doesn't like to talk about the past so he can concentrate on the future but he does recall the time he was chased down the street by a man firing a gun at him. One bullet whizzed near his head but he wasn't struck so, in remembering that, he thinks, "God spared me then and, as long as I keep trying, God keeps helping me."

Dear Lord, sometimes "old" recipes have the tastiest results. Thanks for the "senior seniors" who keep on keeping on! And, Lord, help the ones who have poor health and can no longer function without a lot of medical and physical care. Bless them, Lord, bless them. And reach out your loving hand to them so they will know that no matter how old they are, you still see them and love them as your children.

WE LIVE ON
A LOT OF HOPE

When she was a young girl, Georgia Adams had one goal in life. She says, "I just always wanted to be a mother." And she did that! After working for a couple of years as a secretary in a job where she met a lot of interesting people, she left the business world, got married, and had nine children. Today, she says her one goal in life is for all those children to go to church regularly. Georgia groans, "Some do and some don't, so my husband and I pray about that and we live on a lot of hope."

Through the years, while being a busy mother and parish worker, Georgia has become the ultimate homemaker. Now, after fifty years of marriage, she is still always redoing her house. She loves to make new curtains, rearrange furniture, switch rooms, and change pictures. And when she isn't redecorating, she's trying a new recipe. She says, "I used to have to cook whatever the kids liked. Now I can be more adventurous and it's really fun."

In addition to cooking, sewing, crocheting, and babysitting for twenty-two grandchildren and ten great-grandchildren, she's still busy with parish work. For years, she was in charge of their weekly fish fry (which was very popular and a huge job to coordinate) but now she works with the Ladies Sodality and tutors two children in reading at the parish school. And she is known for always being ready to give a helping hand to any relative or friend who needs one.

Since Georgia's husband retired, he is a willing partner in all her activities but after the hustle-bustle of raising nine children they are a very relaxed, laid-back couple. They now have time to go to daily Mass together every morning and, later, every afternoon at about 4 PM, they always take time out to just sit and talk over a small glass of wine or a snack.

Georgia has noticed that some people are so self-involved that all they think about or talk about is the limitations of aging. But she says, "If you think of others and try to help them, you don't have time to think about yourself. We know it can't last forever but right now, we're as busy as ever—and hope it doesn't change."

Dear Lord, all the famous movie stars and politicians grab the headlines but people like Georgia and her husband are the ones who make the world go 'round. They quietly live good lives, work hard, enjoy every day in spite of difficulties or hardships, and pray for their children to have lives as happy as theirs has been. It hasn't been easy with so many children and a limited income but they made it. And now they live on a lot of hope for the future. And, Lord, after fifty years, they still make it a point to have a quiet "time-out" every afternoon together. Now that's a miracle!

The ordinary arts we practice every day at home are
of more importance to the soul than their simplicity
might suggest. THOMAS MOORE

A seventy-five-year-old woman diagnosed with terminal cancer said to her friend, "My life is going to be over and all I've been is just a housewife and mother." And her friend replied, "What could possibly be more important than that! Look at all your children and grandchildren who are devoted to you because you've been such an important influence in their lives. You've taught them morals and principles to live by but you've also been a lot of fun and given them memories they will cherish forever. What greater good could you have accomplished?" What greater good indeed. Ordinary arts. Food for the soul. A legacy that will live on for generations.

FROM
SUBURBAN PRIEST
TO URBANITE

Father Joe came into the restaurant wearing a furry Russian-style hat, a bulky snow-day jacket, and a big smile. A few years before, he had retired at age seventy-five from his work as pastor of a very large, very busy suburban parish. Our paths hadn't crossed much since, so it was good to see him again and hear how retirement had changed his lifestyle of many years.

When he left the parish, I was surprised to hear that, instead of moving to another parish as a senior priest in residence or going to our very nice local residence for retired priests, he moved into a city apartment. Father explained that about a third of the retired priests in the area choose this type of retirement living and he felt he was lucky to find an apartment in a friendly little neighborhood that is only ten minutes from each of his three sisters' urban homes.

This frees him to spend time with them (since they too are getting older), still be active as a priest, and also have some free time. (He said that now he can go to a concert, relax, and enjoy it instead of falling asleep because he has had such a stressful day and will have to be up and ready to go by 6 AM.)

Father said he loves being a priest but, as pastor, he was "on call" most days from early morning Mass to late evening when he might finally be able to sit down and watch the ten o'clock news. He was beginning to have some health problems and decided it was time to change to some "less scheduled" days, with fewer responsibilities. He had been at his last parish for sixteen years and enjoyed the work and the parishioners but it was a long time for such long days and he was afraid he might "start getting grumpy."

Now he is doing what he calls "supply work"—weddings, funerals, saying Mass for a group of nuns at a nearby hospital whenever the chaplain is not available, filling in when parish priests need an extra hand, and giving talks about the book he finally found time to write.

Father Joe always enjoyed traveling and took many far-and-near trips with fellow priests, and now he is "traveling" again—going to different parishes, meeting different people, wherever and whenever he is needed. As a liturgist, he is interested to see how parish worship services may differ a bit liturgically from place to place and finds the changes very positive. He also continues to meet with an ecumenical group of ministers and participate in a rabbi-priest dialogue.

He remembers the very busy days when he would spend early morning time between Masses walking back and forth inside or outside the church, with his book, praying the office. This way, he knew parishioners would be hesitant to disturb his morning prayer and he would get some privacy and some exercise too! Now he is enjoying being a "supply" man, and his doctor is happy to see that Father Joe's roaming retirement has given him better health and lower blood pressure.

Dear Lord, I never thought about a priest doing "supply work" but I was well aware that they are truly "service men." We are so grateful to have the kind of service men who protect our country, supply our groceries, keep our electricity working, and repair our temperamental computers. But the most important ones are those who service our souls. Thank you, Lord, for their self-sacrificing lives and bless them all in their roaming retirements.

A "MODEL" FOR AGING

Believe it or not, even glamorous, thin, perfect profes-sional models have birthdays. But it isn't often that one of them is still appearing in national advertising cam-paigns after a seventieth birthday! It does happen though because I recently read about a popular model who lives in a Park Avenue apartment and says she's been up, down, rich, poor but is "still here." She has always used just one name in her career so let's call her Sylvia.

According to a newspaper interview, Sylvia says people should not think her life has been all glamour. As with most career women, she has had to put in a lot of work and use a lot of discipline to still be working, still getting assignments to pose for a fashion ad in New York or fly to Paris to walk the runway in a designer's show.

She says, "I live a real life but when I show up for work, I have to look like and act like a model." She admits that life is a challenge but says she has "the courage, strength, and enough good health to see the positive."

Sylvia was "discovered" and appeared in a Vogue ad when she was a teenager. Since then, she has posed for many famous photographers. One of them said of her, "She has always been comfortable with being herself and whenever she comes to a shoot, she's in a good mood and a joy to work with."

Pictured with perfectly but simply styled white hair and an understated but colorful outfit, she says, "I've always been tall, skinny, and angular and sometimes that look was not popular but now it seems to be in fashion so I'm considered beautiful at seventy and I hope that empowers older women. I'm afraid there are many women who are not enjoying their later years as much as they could and I challenge them to feel good about themselves as long as they live. I've learned to forgive myself and others. If I make a mistake, I don't dwell on it. I just try to do better the next time."

She admits that part of aging well is luck but she is careful to exercise, eat healthy, and get plenty of sleep. She also admits that probably a big part of her "luck" was inheriting good genes from her mother who was a Broadway dancer and was still doing well at the age of ninety.

A longtime friend says of Sylvia, "She's fun and inspiring but the most endearing thing about her is that she's so friendly and easy to get along with, you forgive her for being so gorgeous."

Sylvia herself said, "Most people in the world are really good and I know the difference now. That's what's wonderful about being seventy. I'm so grateful for the friends who haven't died on me. And I'm furious with the ones who did."

Dear Lord, I know what she means. I'm furious with the few friends who left too soon and are no longer available for me to call to chat or stop by for a visit. But I'm grateful to have so many friends still in my life. They're not all tall, angular, and glamorous as a model but they are all pretty cute and friendly and easy to get along with and, with your help, Lord, they're trying to be models of aging well by enjoying these later years. Thanks, Lord, for all of them.

AN "EVENT-FULL" LIFE

Keeping track of "The Event of the Day" is a senior pick-me-up dreamed up by eighty-year-old Clark McShane.

He says the sun shining through his hilltop bedroom window usually wakes him by 7 AM and his first thought might be, "Now what will be today's 'Event of the Day'?" He might think, "Oh yes, it's Tuesday so I will be picking up the granddaughters after school and we might just order pizza for dinner." Or he might remember, "Oh yes, today is when my Missouri cousin is flying here for a visit."

Some days get off to an early routine start and Clark might not think about the "event" until late in the day. Then he may decide, "It was that story on the evening news. I'm going to follow up and get more details on that." Or something simple like, "Those peaches I found at the Farmer's Market today were the best this year."

Whatever the day brings, Clark always finds a noteworthy "event" and this way he can remind himself—and others—that he leads a very "eventful life!"

And he HAS had an eventful life—marriage, children he loves, grandchildren he dotes on, and now a very comfortable home that catches the sun on a California hilltop. He says he always cautions younger folks to "plan now for your retirement years." He warns them that people are living longer today so it is more necessary than in the past to plan financially, physically, and mentally for life in the "golden years."

Although his mother died when he was only seven, he has many happy memories of days with Dad. He remembers feeling very special, riding to church on Sunday in his dad's 1936 Dodge. One year the pastor challenged families to try to come every Sunday for a year without missing a single Sunday. When Clark and his Dad met the challenge, they each received a lapel pin. His Dad's pin had the name of the church but Clark's pin simply had the word, "honor." He treasured that pin.

Clark recalls when he was a teenager and loved to go to the movies, all the movies were rated G. From kids to grandmas, the whole family could find a movie to enjoy. He says most of today's movies should be rated G for Gross. In those teen years, Clark loved music and thought he might pursue a musical career OR become an executive in a nice big office. He did achieve that executive dream and he still keeps a baby grand piano in his home so he can play a tune and maybe even sing along as part of one of his eventful days.

Dear Lord, what a great idea—to be aware and grateful and excited enough to look about and find one best thing each and every day. It's so easy to overlook all the delightful little things in an ordinary life, all the reasons to be glad to be alive. Lord, you spread the banquet, you shower us with treasures. Help us be wise enough to recognize and appreciate the "events" of our days.

To grow older is a new venture in itself.

GOETHE

*I*t seems that Goethe practiced what he preached because it has been reported that he wrote almost all of the second part of *Faust* between the ages of seventy-three and eighty-two—quite a venture! But then Goethe probably couldn't have identified with "growing older" in today's world. He was a genius who lived in the court of a duke from the time he was twenty-six years old, so he wouldn't have had to grocery shop or try to get the plumbing repaired or battle with an HMO to pay for an oxygen tank. He also didn't have a supermarket offering strawberries in the winter and ice cream in the summer. He didn't have indoor plumbing or a way to get an oxygen tank when he really needed one. So enthusiasm for life crosses all boundaries. It helps move above and beyond troubling trifles and also helps look inside to find spiritual solace. Changing a lifestyle, facing illness, learning to be patient with someone else or with yourself—none of these are easy but with prayer and enthusiasm they can still be adventures!

DON'T BE AFRAID

Anyone fortunate enough to be in the audience (as I once was) to hear Richard John Neuhaus speak was fortunate indeed. When Father Neuhaus died in 2009, many articles appeared about his amazing life as a theologian and writer, the stages of his life from a liberal Lutheran minister to a conservative Catholic priest, and his views on death.

He was no stranger to death because, as a young minister, he worked in the death ward at Kings County Hospital. This was a large room that housed fifty to a hundred people who were dying. He was with two or three people each day as they died. One of them, just as he was dying, said to Father, with joy, "Ohhh! Don't be afraid."

Some years later, Father had his own near-death experience when an undiagnosed condition led to a series of operations, an extended stay in ICU, and a very long recovery. While in the hospital, one night he knew he was lying flat but suddenly he felt he was sitting up, staring into the darkness where he "saw but didn't see" two presences who somehow conveyed to him the message: "Everything is ready." He never forgot this experience and spoke about it and wrote about it in one of his books.

Later, when he was partly recovered from his illness, he wrote, "After some time, I could shuffle the few blocks to church and say Mass. At the altar, I cried a lot and hoped the people didn't notice. To think that I'm really here after all, I thought, at the altar, at the *axis mundi*, the center of life. And of death."

Father went on to spend many years in God's ministry, writing, lecturing, teaching, taking God's message to millions. He wrote and edited nearly thirty books and founded the journal *First Things*, in which he wrote a monthly column. In his last column, after he had been diagnosed with cancer, he wrote "Be assured that I neither fear to die nor refuse to live. If it is to die, all that has been is but a slight intimation of what is to be. If it is to live, there is much I hope to do in the interim."

Dear Lord, we live in the interim so we must live it to its fullness, remembering there is much to do while rejoicing in the dying patient's words, "Do not be afraid." Help us, Lord, to faithfully intermingle the remembering and the rejoicing.

WHEN ONE HUNDRED IS A PLUS

Recently there have been surprisingly many one-hundred-year-olds appearing in the news—and I'd like to tell you about two of them. Let's call them Joe Jones and John Smith.

John, a famous classical music composer, spent his hundredth birthday attending a concert at Carnegie Hall. One of his compositions was on the program and it was not one he had composed in his thirties or fifties or seventies. He wrote it when he was ninety-eight years old. In fact, once he turned ninety, at a time when most people would definitely be slowing down, he had a new burst of creativity and completed more than forty published works.

A well-known conductor says John is "still writing at the top of his form. Like other great composers, every time he writes a piece, he has new ideas he's trying, as well as coming up with a subtler reworking of something he had done before."

John says that when he was younger he was exploring what he would like to write. Sometimes he would spend a year writing a major piece of music. Now his works are shorter. He explains, "I have done all my great big noisy pieces. Now I write simpler ones and that is an adventure."

John still lives in the apartment he shared with his wife who fiercely protected him until her death a few years ago. Now a small group of musicians "keep an eye" on him and he has an aide and a business manager who look after everything from his finances to his hearing aids.

Every day, John wakes at 7 AM and composes for two hours. Then he goes out with an aide for a "constitutional" walk. He rests after lunch, then composes again or welcomes visitors. And in the evening, he listens to Mozart or watches French satellite TV—unless he's going out for a concert.

In contrast, Joe lives in a retirement home that he finds "a comfortable yet stimulating" environment. He celebrated his hundredth birthday at a party for the residents there plus a second party hosted by his son and daughter-in-law for family and friends. He said "it was a big party with lots of celebrating."

Joe remembers another celebration when he was a kid—the ending of the First World War! He says the kids celebrated by dragging and banging pots and pans on the sidewalk.

Joe remembers riding the streetcar, happy family reunions at a local park, and the years with his wife and daughter who are both deceased. He says his son is now seventy-one, so he's already old enough himself to qualify for the retirement home. Joe is very happy there where he plays poker with a group once a week and fills in occasionally for a pinochle or scrabble game.

Joe has been an altar boy, a church usher, a plumber's helper, and a thirty-year postal employee. He says when people ask him for advice about how to have successful retirement years, he tells them, "Just take it easy—one day at a time. I never worried about getting old or anything else." Then he adds, "Prayer is also very important." He says he prays every day—"the usual prayers, you know."

These two centenarians have led very different lives but they both have found retirement routines that work just right for them.

Dear Lord, one hundred years is a long time to stay busy and productive and contented. But more and more seniors have reached or are approaching that milestone. The conductor noted that John's music is still "new" because he is often trying "a subtler reworking of some things done before." In the same way, these two very different gentlemen have subtly reworked their lives and found a comfortable retirement. Lord, please help other seniors learn to subtly rework old ways to become easier new ways. And remind us all, Lord, to take Joe's advice to worry less and pray every day.

IT'S A CAPITOL IDEA!

When asked how she felt about having a fiftieth birthday and becoming eligible for some senior discounts, Jane Amberson reacted with "shock and awe." She said, "I actually never thought about getting older. And, as for retirement, my husband says he is never going to retire, so I didn't need to think about that either."

Then she recalls, "When I was taking care of four babies and there was always 'one more thing to do,' I once thought that maybe when we became senior citizens, my husband and I might get one of those small motor homes and just travel around, relaxing and seeing the country. Now I guess we'll have to think of something else." And why would that be? "Well," she said, "we've already visited forty-six of the fifty states and also took trips to Canada and Ireland."

She then explained that years ago, her family visited a relative in Columbus, Ohio, and there weren't many sights to see there so he showed them the state capitol building.

Her husband photographed it, and this led to an unusual hobby. He decided it would be fun to visit and photograph every state capitol—and they've been doing that on vacations ever since.

Jane says she guesses her own hobby must be volunteering. Whenever anyone needs help, their first thought is to call on Jane. She has done every kind of job and held every kind of office for organizations at her church and her children's schools. She has been a Girl Scout leader for twenty years, working with girls from kindergarten through twelfth grade. Jane not only gets every job done but done well! She says she loves all the activities and never ever gets bored. She is particularly glad to volunteer for church activities because "I think of our parish as my extended family."

Jane has done a bit of scrapbooking and made beautiful albums of their travel photographs—plus, like most travelers, she has a box of photos waiting to be put in more albums. She says her role models are her parents. Her mother is a long-time parish volunteer who often works side-by-side with Jane. A favorite retirement activity of her parents is to join Jane and her husband on their capitol trips.

Jane says she has heard about and might begin to worry a bit about the Empty Nest Syndrome since the last of her four daughters is a senior in high school and will soon leave for college like her sisters. The house will be quieter but Jane will probably be as busy as ever because, with her volunteer reputation, there will always be someone calling to ask, "Could you possibly help with…."

Dear Lord, thank you for all the workers who keep organizations going and make special events special for others. And, Lord, please encourage seniors to not be too shy or "age-sensitive" to offer their help. Plenty of church, school, or civic organizations have budgets too small today to hire enough workers and would welcome some "retired" helping hands.

KEEPING TRACK
OF THE "KIDS"

Around the time Orville Wright made his first brief flight, Teddy Roosevelt was serving a second term as president, and eggs were selling for twenty-seven cents a dozen, Delia Sanders celebrated her first birthday. A couple of years ago, she celebrated her hundredth birthday, and today she says it's God's will that her senses are still sharp and her spirit strong.

According to a newspaper interview, she tries to keep it that way through daily exercise for her mind, the love and care of good friends, and staying in touch with the "kids" who were her students when she was an English and journalism teacher for many years.

Delia's idea of mind exercise is to read three newspapers every morning, work the *New York Times* crossword puzzle, and watch *Jeopardy* on TV every afternoon. And every Sunday, she "attends" church services by listening to the radio or watching TV, because she is no longer able to be involved with the parish activities that were formerly an important part of her life.

As a child she loved reading and always took a book wherever she went. When she worked on her high school newspaper she got interested in journalism, which led to her career as an English teacher. Now one of her greatest joys is keeping up with her former students—she calls them her "kids" although some are almost eighty years old! They all have fond memories of the educational influence she had on them. One recalled, "She was so talented, always well-respected, and very knowledgeable about the ways and wiles of her students." Another mentioned her husband, Bill, who was a science teacher and said, "They were a real team."

Delia and Bill liked to travel, visit Civil War sites, and vacation in Florida. Today, with the help of caretakers, Delia still lives in the home she shared with her husband. She still tears up when she talks about his achievements and his death after sixty years of marriage. And she smiles when she talks about her "kids."

Dear Lord, thank you for so many good teachers who have made a practical and spiritual impact on students and influenced the way their lives have unfolded. Thank you for all the teachers in my life who taught me about values and writing and spirituality and fun. And thank you for the new people I keep meeting and how they each reach and teach me by the example of their own lives. Looking back, I realize how many times you sent people to teach me your lessons. Looking forward, I am excited to see whom you might send next and what lessons I may still keep learning—even if I should live as long as Delia!

We don't receive wisdom; we must discover it for
ourselves after a journey that no one can take for us
or spare us.   MARCEL PROUST

$\mathcal{E}$ ach person journeys alone, even when surrounded by friends or family. And each leg of the journey, each detour, each rest stop, each disappointment or discovery alters the original trip plan. Wisdom isn't a gift. You have to live a lot, learn a lot, sometimes take the less-traveled path, sometimes dare to welcome adventure, and pray a lot as you seek to earn that elusive wisdom. Age can add a lot of wrinkles on the "map" of your journey but you can just pretend they are simply squiggly lines put there by a life of experience. So just keep trudging along even without the help of a modern "global positioning device" and enjoy every minute as you hope and pray for a happy landing.

A BIG MAN
—IN EVERY WAY

Father Nick Morris has always been big (very tall and a bit wide) and he has had a *big* life. His career as a priest included serving as pastor/founder of missions in Brazil, as a pastor of a large midwestern church, and as the editor of a popular Catholic magazine. He has criss-crossed the country preaching homilies to tell about the magazine and get new subscribers, has written many articles, books, and columns, served as president of the Catholic Press Association, and won their prestigious St. Francis de Sales Award. And he has always been known to tell the *biggest*, funniest jokes and stories.

At ninety-two, he never has completely retired. He continued to officiate at endless weddings (and enjoyed them all) and to give talks or homilies at endless gatherings. And he loved to travel for fun with his two sisters and to play golf with his "army" of friends.

Then, a few years ago, he began to have back problems that led to a leg problem so serious that the leg had to be amputated. This slowed him down a bit, but he got a *big* artificial leg and learned how to use it and how to transfer himself into a car so he could continue to go lunching with friends. He also continued to write books and a monthly column for that Catholic magazine.

Just recently, the other leg got into trouble and it too had to be amputated. He told the surgeon, "Be sure to cut it so it's the same length as my other stub. Otherwise, I might not be able to tap dance!"

He no longer towers over everyone with his height but he continues to tower over any gathering with his personality, jokes, and big chuckles at other's jokes.

When I told him he was the first one I had interviewed who was living in a nursing home, he said "You must remember that this is not an ordinary nursing home. It is a religious community."

He went on to explain that they are a Redemptorist family. He said each priest has his own private room and bath (and Father N.'s is full of books and decorated with great memorabilia) but they all go to Mass each morning together, have their meals together, celebrate birthdays or any special occasion—and they are all together at every funeral. It is not just a nursing home. It is a health care center where they are cared for and care about each other.

Father says that aging is a "vocation within a vocation" and cites a Redemptorist Constitution that states "…this profession of vows makes all Redemptorists truly missionaries, whether they are engaged in different activities of the apostolic ministry or are hindered from working at all...their life of prayer, the experience they have acquired, and the services they are still able to render can be a source of inspiration to the younger confreres."

Father N. told how often young and old work together in religious communities so the young learn early to see the elders as role models and to realize that the dignity of a person must always be respected and revered. He admits that even in a community, there will be some elders who see illness and old age as something to be only tolerated and endured, while others seem never to grow "old." Even if they become "decrepit," they continue to be alert and aware and still think young.

Father N. says religious, like all retirees, may fear age will mean losing status, being "put on the shelf," or having to learn to take a back seat. He says that's why they should plan ahead and find a simple hobby or special interest—take an Internet course, trace family history, read about the cultures of other countries, etc. If they do that, they can take the advice of gerontologists who suggest that every reasonably healthy retired person should spend two to four hours every day at some productive and meaningful work that does not require too much exertion.

Father N. has taken that advice himself by continuing writing and being a big inspiration and help to other writers (including me.) He and all the Redemptorists have their own role model, their founder, St. Alphonsus, who wrote much, endured much, and lived to be ninety-one.

Dear Lord, I think Father Nick—and many other elders—epitomize that anonymous quote, "Youth is a gift of nature; age is a work of art." Thank you for them all and teach us to follow their very big examples of spirituality, accomplishment, and joy.

THE MOON ON A SNOWY NIGHT

She's the proverbial "favorite aunt." She delights all the children with surprise trips and gifts, has the holiday parties at her home, helps make arrangements for an annual camping-out week for her brothers, sisters, and offspring. But there's much more to her story.

Deborah Adams is a clinical pharmacist at a major metropolitan hospital complex, writes articles for medical journals, and occasionally gives talks or presentations to groups of doctors. And when I spoke with her recently, she was just back from a getaway trip with her sister and six women friends (ages thirty to sixty) who bravely rented a mountain cabin that was so remote they had to ski to get there. They dragged in all their food, provisions, and implements by toboggan, and one lady added to the "coolness" by bringing along a sled carrying a keg of icy "spirited" drinks!

There was time for fun, taking turns cooking, reading, cross-country skiing, and being awed by the breathtaking scenery with fresh snow everywhere, but no other people anywhere—except for a park ranger who occasionally dropped by on a skimobile to check on them. One of the highlights was the complete quiet of the night with a startlingly bright moon reflecting off a nearby river. All was right with God's world.

But a few years ago, all was not right with Deborah's world. Her father was seriously ill. She was constantly running back and forth to her parents' home and trying to monitor his symptoms and treatments, since she was familiar with the medical world. She had been living in a condo near her work but she sold it and told a realtor to find her a house. She only had two criteria: it had to be near her parents' home and close to a major highway so she could quickly get back and forth to work.

She says she felt fortunate she could do this because her job was secure and she could rearrange her work hours. She was also single, without the family obligations of her seven brothers and sisters. She knew her Dad was ready to die but his family was not ready to let him go. For this reason, she encouraged trying "everything" for a year of in-and-out hospital stays. In retrospect, she thinks maybe that was not best.

A few years later, when her mother was ill, Deborah was more protective and refused to agree to treatments she felt her mother was too weak to withstand. There were multiple emergencies and major decisions to be made about care but she was able to keep her mother comfortable and at home most of the time for a couple of years. Her family helped out in every way possible and were grateful to Deborah for all she did.

Now Deborah is grateful she moved from the condo to a house where she has a lovely garden and often gives friends gifts of the flowers she grows. Her brother and his sons mow the lawn and do repairs for her. And soon Deborah is planning to go back to school to get another degree to further her career. And she is also hoping she might get to visit that cabin in the Tetons again next year— where the moon is amazingly bright on snowy mountain nights.

Dear Lord, thank you for all the children who care so well for their parents, and thanks for the parents who care so well for their children.

A DOCTOR'S PRESCRIPTION
FOR AGING

When you meet this tall, quiet man, the lilt in his step, the twinkle in his eye, and his beaming smile give you a hint of how much he really loves life. And what a life he's led! He's been an Air Force captain, a consultant for an astronaut program, the head of cardiology and pulmonary care in a large hospital, and now, at eighty, he's the deepest voice in a barbershop quartet! But he's quick to tell you, "The Lord moved me in everything I did. He always led the way—and he still does."

After his stint as an Air Force doctor, Eric Anderson served as a consultant on the altitude chamber of Project Mercury and had dinner with some of the astronauts we've all heard about like John Glenn and Gus Grissom. In addition to specializing in cardiology, he headed a hospital education program designed to keep doctors intellectually active and up-to-date on recent medical discoveries. And, for many years he was a compassionate presence in the lives of the many patients he treated.

Eric had a very heavy workload and would often come home to have dinner with his wife and children but then go to his desk to do paperwork afterward. He felt being a doctor was a privilege and he loved it all, but it was exhausting and he knew when it was time to move on.

Now, he is truly relishing retirement. Some years ago, he had been dragged, kicking and protesting, to a Bible study group, but after a few sessions he became a true Bible student. Since then, praying with Scripture has helped him through difficult times. And now, as a retiree, he can spend an hour every day with the Bible. He is delighted that he can also have time to start a project and finish it. And he can even take time to scrub between his toes! (Eric laughingly says this is a new luxury for him because he always had to take quick showers to race off to work but now he even has time for toes!)

Another important part of Eric's retirement years has been working with the Salvation Army. A few years ago, he went to a meeting and heard a talk by a Salvation Army general that so impressed him, he asked if he could volunteer to ring a bell at Christmas. Instead, within four months, he found himself a member of their board. Now he heads a spiritual growth program for the Salvation Army and spends two days a week leading a Bible study group for men addicted to drugs and alcohol. He says when he was a doctor, he saw most of his patients get well but it doesn't work that way with these addicts. Many relapse, and he has had to learn not to be discouraged but he keeps at it, hoping and persevering.

Persevering has always been one of his traits. Even as a kid, Eric was a baseball nut but was never good enough to make the team. He kept at it, practicing at every opportunity, and by college he had improved enough that he once hit two home runs in one game!

Eric says he was never at the top of the class in school either. He was a "middle" student but when it came to getting into a special medical program, there were five thousand applicants for eighty-five spots and he made the cut. He says he wishes he could tell those on college admission boards today to sometimes take a closer look at those "middle" students.

This "middle" man has certainly risen to the top. He is still serving others but has time now for fun—like singing with his barbershop group, playing tennis, and even hitting the ski slopes at the age of eighty. He is still loving life and going wherever the Lord leads.

Dear Lord, it's a real joy to spend time with such a friend of yours. Thanks for all such doctors and for all your friends who work so hard in so many ways in your vineyard. And thanks especially for the retirees who recognize and appreciate the blessings and delights of senior life, the surprising places you lead them, and, yes, Lord, for the time you give them for singing and skiing and toe scrubs.

Self-reverence, self-knowledge, self-control. These three alone lead life to sovereign power.

ALFRED, LORD TENNYSON

Sovereign power? Hmmm. Was Tennyson talking about the life of a king or an individual? The dictionary indicates sovereign could mean "exercising supreme power over a limited sphere." Well, "self" is definitely a limited sphere. So let's start with self-control, always a touchy subject. Theoretically, by the time you get to be a senior, you should have learned how to do this. But who has—really? And self-reverence? Certainly seniors reverence life but they still sometimes eat stuff like donuts or hamburgers—not a good way to reverence the body—but who's perfect? So that leaves self-knowledge. Even seniors do so much multi-tasking today, they might have lots of titles—moms, dads, nurturers, breadwinners, caregivers, caretakers, educators, organizers, couch potatoes. Well, the list varies with each person so who are you really? True knowledge of self probably takes more than a lifetime. Maybe all seniors can do is ponder this quote and hope it will lead to accepting the mystery of the sovereignty of God.

WHAT'S IN A NAME?

Senior Citizens? How about Seasoned Citizens? Or OWLS (Older, Wiser, Livelier Souls)? Or Sage Ager, Geri-Actives, OPALS (Older persons with Active Life Styles), Age of Dignity, or the X-Y-Z Group (eXtra Years of Zest)? Now that an AARP discount can begin at fifty and people are living longer active lives, the tag of elderly is being replaced with lots of new names. Later years are not always all rosy, with health or financial problems, but for many, they can be a new beginning, a time to re-invent their lives.

In today's fast-changing world, many may choose to—or have to—start a new career. One midlife lady executive whose job was "downsized" sent out many resumes with no result. Then, a young working couple who were friends asked if she could possibly "work" for them as a babysitter temporarily while she was job-hunting. As a favor to them, she agreed and went to work in sweats instead of high heels and spent days in the fresh air at the park or doing the usual child-care activities—which meant seeing the world with the new eyes of youth. After a while, she looked better, felt better, and was happier than she had been as a stressed-out executive. Fortunately, her husband still had a job and salary so they could downsize their expenses—and she had found a new career as a nanny!

Other almost-seniors have reevaluated their lives and found new interests that led to a more fulfilling lifestyle—physically, intellectually, or spiritually. But this is not the first generation to make dramatic changes or great accomplishments past midlife. Here are just a few of the plus-fifty notables:

> *Clara Barton* was a teacher, a clerk, and then a nurse. For her nursing work during the Civil War, she was dubbed the "Angel of the Battlefield." She was fifty-one when she founded the American Red Cross.

> *Juliette Gordon Low* was a Savannah-born socialite and widow when she met the founder of the British Boy Scouts and was so impressed by his ideas that, in 1912, she recruited eighteen girls and began what was to become the world's largest educational organization for girls—the Girl Scouts of America.

> *Abraham Lincoln* was a small-town lawyer who got into politics, won the presidential election when he was fifty-one and has inspired generations.

Walt Disney was a cartoonist who parlayed his talent and imagination into an industry and was fifty-four when the first Disneyland amusement park opened in 1955.

Clare Boothe Luce was already a journalist and Broadway playwright when she decided to run for Congress and won. She represented Connecticut from 1943 to 1947. And then, at the age of fifty, she went to Italy to become the first woman to serve as U.S. Ambassador to a major nation.

Julia Child was a young graduate from Smith who wanted to be a spy so she worked during World War II for the OSS (the forerunner of the CIA.) Then she married a diplomat, learned to cook, and, at the age of fifty-one, became the star of her own TV show, *The French Chef.*

Mary Kay Ash had a desk job when a man she had trained was promoted above her, at twice her salary! Mary Kay had the nerve to quit her job and start her own business. When she was fifty, her "Mary Kay Cosmetics" had sales of more than $1 million and became one of the world's largest direct sellers of skin care products.

Winston Churchill had quite a career as a British statesman but was sixty-six when he became England's prime minister and proved to be an inspiring wartime leader in WWII.

Nelson Mandela, a South African statesman, spent twenty-seven years in prison because of his struggle against apartheid but finally became president of South Africa at the age of seventy-six.

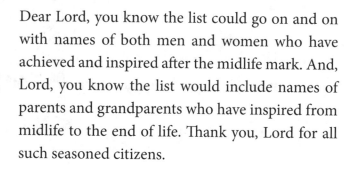

Dear Lord, you know the list could go on and on with names of both men and women who have achieved and inspired after the midlife mark. And, Lord, you know the list would include names of parents and grandparents who have inspired from midlife to the end of life. Thank you, Lord for all such seasoned citizens.

A TUTOR, PRAYER PARTNER, AND EUCHARISTIC MINISTER
—NOT THE IMAGE OF A LITTLE OLD LADY!

In her very quiet, unobtrusive way, Sister Margaret says, "I know I'm living in a retirement center and I'll soon be eighty-five but somehow, I still find it hard to think of myself as a 'little old lady.'"

After many years of teaching, first as full-time, then part-time, she realized it was time to let go and see where God would send her next. She still drives a car, ferrying other Sisters on short jaunts, and she has found many retirement outlets. She delights in being part of a group of volunteers who tutor one student each year at a grade school through a program whose goal is not so much to teach as to offer support and encouragement to a child who is struggling in either scholastic or social skills.

The class teacher selects a child who will spend an hour once a week in private time with a tutor. The teacher tells the tutor what to stress to help the child become more confident or motivated or maybe just to feel like someone really cares enough about him or her to spend that extra time each week. This wonderful program has been a great source of accomplishment, both for teachers AND for tutors. And Sister Margaret loves it.

Each year, she is also a "prayer partner" with a children's class at the nearby Catholic elementary school. The children pray for her each day and she prays for them. She also may read them an inspirational story, bring them a little treat of cookies or a holy card, or tell them a story from her life.

One item she shared with them was a holy card with a picture of a beautiful little child and the words "Would you like to adopt me spiritually?" On the back is a prayer to "spiritually" adopt an unborn child, praying its life might be spared. The children loved to say that prayer and their teacher extended the idea by having a class baby shower, inviting the class to bring baby gifts to be taken to a shelter for unwed mothers.

Then, not to leave out the adults, Sister is also a Eucharistic minister and takes communion to those in a nearby hospital/nursing home.

Sister happily recalls the places where she taught, including a mission in New Mexico, and the years when she had to keep going to summer school to finally get her degree—and then spent the next summer *teaching* summer school!

She remembers when she first planned to enter the convent and was told to get a physical. The family doctor checked her out and then said, "You are disgustingly healthy." Although she has had the usual aches and pains of age and one recent minor operation, she has fortunately continued to be as the doctor described. Through the years, Sister has done a lot of teaching and learning and, evidently, she plans to keep it up since she recently completed a several-week course about the spirituality of aging!

 Dear Lord, thanks for helping me keep meeting so many great role models. At a certain age, we are all tempted to think we already know all we need to know—and maybe some things we wish we didn't know! But spirituality, Lord. I guess we can never learn enough about that mysteriously wonderful subject. Or maybe it's just me. I know I need to go to summer school and winter school and the school of hard knocks, and there will always be something new waiting around the corner to teach me since I am still at the kindergarten level when it comes to your subject—spirituality. Thank you, Lord, for being so inscrutable that I can always look forward to being surprised by your wonders.

WHO, WHAT, WHEN, WHY?

Geraldine Winters really loved her job and her life, so when someone asked her what she thought about retirement, her response was immediate. She said, "Who would want to retire—and why?" Then she added, "What would you do without the organization of a daily work schedule, the give-and-take of coworkers and, of course, the money? And how would you know when it was time to go?" But today she has found answers to all those questions and says, "I couldn't imagine why anyone would want to retire but now I can't imagine why I waited so long to do it!"

Since she has always been an organized person, she has scheduled her retirement days with volunteer work, enjoys the give-and-take of the new friends she has made with those "jobs," and still keeps in touch with some former coworkers. She also has time to shop for bargains, save grocery coupons, etc., so the money stretches far enough. And with all of this, she has discovered the taste of freedom—the ability to be spontaneous and to be the one to choose how to use each day.

On a whim, she can invite people over for an informal evening get-together for coffee and dessert or dips and drinks, or she can go out to a late movie without worrying about having to get up early the next morning. She can go to a three-day spiritual retreat without having to use "vacation days." And she is even more careful about her health, getting regular checkups, etc., since it's easier to schedule appointments and she has more time to plan a healthy diet instead of dashing through the drive-through after work.

She volunteers at the zoo and the local tourist information center, gets involved with lots of church activities, and feels she is helping others while enjoying every minute of it.

She says this has been a good lesson for her. It's so easy to fear the unknown, to decide ahead of time that something will be too disagreeable to even consider—and then discover it to be a very happy surprise. Geraldine realizes how blessed she is and knows that, this time, giving up a good thing has led to something even better.

Dear Lord, although retirement has not been as rosy for some as it has been for Geraldine, it's been a rewarding time for many. The other day I saw a lady wearing a T-shirt with a large word in red— "RETIRED"—but beneath that in smaller print, it read, "I was tired yesterday and I'm tired again today." Well, I could identify with that but only because there are so many good senior possibilities, I want to try them all—and that can get you tired! Thank you, Lord, for all the jokes and all the puns about coming of "age." As long as we keep laughing at ourselves instead of others, we can grin and bear it!

Just like home—You don't always get what you want!

SIGN IN AN OLD-TIME
HOME-TOWN RESTAURANT

*W*hen you're a kid and decide what you want to be when you grow up, you don't always get what you want—or what you planned. The same is true of aging. You may have planned well for retirement but then circumstances beyond your control came into your life and you didn't get what you wanted. Or maybe you got something even better!

Just like home—sometimes what you want is not what you need or what will bring you the greatest blessings.

SMILE
—IKE'S TAKING YOUR PICTURE

Whenever there's a special occasion, you can usually count on there being flowers, music, maybe posters or balloons—and cameras. For many years, whenever there was a major Catholic event in a large Missouri city, you could count on there being the flowers and music—and a Hasselblad.

The Hasselblad was a heavy professional expensive camera made in Sweden with a German lens that was the constant companion of Ike Walters. Ike was everywhere with his camera but, unlike the paparazzi, his was always a quiet unobtrusive presence that never got in the way of the "happening." You never had to stretch your neck to see around Ike and yet he always got the perfect shot. Some of his photos were such great "Kodak moments" that he won several national *Parade* Magazine photo contests.

Ike's interest in photography began when he bought a $1 "Baby Brownie" to take photos of his family and neighborhood. This led to a career that began at a portrait studio, was interrupted when he went overseas with the Army in WWII, resumed when he became a freelance cameraman, and lasted until he was eighty-six years old and finally decided to retire!

Some seniors might be old enough to remember the "Sidewalk Photographer" who would stand on a busy corner and snap pictures of people on the street with the offer to print the film and mail them the photo for a small fee. (Not-yet-seniors might have one of those sidewalk photos of parents or grandparents in the family album.) That's what Ike became when he returned from World War II. In fact, he organized a group of photographers who worked on various downtown streets while he himself set up his tripod at the local theatre and at the ballpark.

After a few years of that, his photos began to win so many of the hometown newspaper's photo contests, he got the attention of a local Catholic newspaper, and for the rest of his career he was their official photographer, traveling to several counties to record every special event. He also took photos for universities, hospitals, and businesses. During that time, he photographed such notables as Pope John Paul II, Dorothy Day, Bob Hope, John F. Kennedy, Mother Teresa, Art Linkletter, and Cardinal Mindszenty. In later years, he switched from the heavy Hasselblad to a Nikon 35mm camera. He won multiple Catholic Press Association awards and worked with several different editors. One of them said, "...he is a consummate professional—a true artist but not a temperamental artist."

When asked about retirement, Ike said you should keep working as long as you can but "you have to retire some time. If I could do it all over again, I would. I enjoyed it all. Every day, every event was different."

Ike and his wife have been loyal members of the same Catholic parish for over forty years and he says he now has time to drive her wherever she wants to go and he still keeps busy but no longer with a camera. He sold all of his camera equipment because "today all the grandchildren have those digital cameras and they send *me* photographs."

Dear Lord, who says there is no such thing as time travel? With old photograph albums or new digital cameras, we can travel back just to yesterday or way back through the years. We can laugh at the funny hairdos, clothes, cars, and expressions, and we can get teary-eyed at all the remember-whens. Thank you, Lord, for photographers like Ike who were there to capture the special events for us. And thanks for all the moms and dads who didn't have a Hasselblad but managed to make so many family events special with or without a camera. Of course, we don't have any pictures of you in those albums, Lord, but we know you were there. We know you were there.

A HIGHLY
REGARDED NAP

Thomas Quigley likes to tell the story about his dad and the skylight. Thomas said that after his mom died, his dad decided it was time to achieve something he had long planned to do—put a skylight in the family room. He was eighty-five years old at the time but felt comfortable on the roof since he always cleaned the gutters. One fine sunny day when he was working, it seemed a fine sunny time for a nap. So he just stretched out on the roof and went to sleep.

Unfortunately, a neighbor's kitchen window had an excellent view of that roof, and when his neighbor saw him, she panicked and put in an emergency call. Soon troops arrived, made a lot of noise climbing the ladder, and Mr. Quigley sat up and said, "Can't a man take a nap on his own roof?"

This is just one of the stories of Dad, who is ninety-six now and still living in that house, enjoying a skylight and managing very well with help from the "Thomas and Jane

Easy-Serve" (his son and daughter-in-law.) One day when they had brought in groceries and done a bit of cleaning, Dad quietly said, "I hope you know I love you." And then he added, "When I grew up in my house, no one ever said that."

Thomas was very touched and realized that, ninety years ago when Dad was growing up, even the happiest families probably didn't say things like that.

Now Thomas himself has retired but no one would know it. He began his career teaching English in a large suburban school district, then continued furthering his own education, got a doctorate in school administration, and moved up through six jobs until he was associate superintendent of schools and had spent thirty-two years in that one school district. By then he felt he had accomplished all his goals and expectations and it was time for someone else to bring in new ideas. He said he didn't want to wait until someone said "Are you still here?" so he took early retirement.

One of the first things he did was to go on a retreat using the Spiritual Exercises of St. Ignatius of Loyola to help decide which of his interests he should pursue next. He soon began teaching part-time at a university and then was asked to serve on the board of a Catholic girls' academy. He gradually delved deeper into spirituality, spending two years at the Aquinas Institute of Theology and receiving a certificate in spiritual direction. After six years on the academy board, he joined and then became chairman of the board of a new middle school for girls from underprivileged families. He helped that school evolve into a successful springboard to prepare girls to continue in higher education. He recently was the guest of honor at an elegant dinner where he was presented with a special achievement award for his many hours of outstanding service to them.

His studies of spirituality next led Thomas to being a formative part of several spiritual programs, and he regularly does individual spiritual counseling to those who come seeking a deeper spirituality in their lives.

But Thomas has always spent plenty of time with his own family of four children and ten grandchildren. When one of his sons graduated from high school, one of the teachers said, "Thomas, I don't know what you did with this boy but whatever it was, you did the right thing."

Thomas and his wife (who also retired from the school district and now volunteers at a school for the deaf) have always enjoyed traveling. They try to take one big trip every other year (like a cruise to Alaska) and lots of little trips in between. He says that whatever he has been able to do for others has been in gratitude for all that he has been given in his life. And it looks like he will continue giving for a long time, since he is obviously not the retiring type—and much too busy to take a nap on his roof.

Dear Lord, thank you for all those like Thomas who give of their time and life to help others seek you and grow in spirituality. And thank you for all the dads who give us memorable stories and remind us that one of the perks of age is to do what you want, when you want—even when you're on top of a house feeling sleepy on a nice warm sunny day.

SUNSHINE, EGGS, AND
MEXICAN
MEMORIES

It seems like a bit of sunshine has swept into the room when Heather Fyle comes in, all dressed in yellow. She's wearing a soft, long skirt patterned with yellow blossoms and a yellow top accented with a dramatic Mexican beaded necklace. She's just back from her annual three-month escape-from-winter, spent in a tiny charming town in Mexico where she meets friends and enjoys weather that's always in the seventies and eighties. She calls "her" town the "Paris of Mexico."

Although she lives in an independent living facility and admits to being eighty-three, Heather says, "I never feel old." She explained, "I guess that's because I'm lucky to have inherited good genes so I'm healthy enough to continue to do all the things I've done for the last forty years."

She says she has always loved sewing and making things, and by the age of seven she had learned to use her mother's treadle sewing machine. Since then, she's been involved in all kinds of crafts. Then, about forty years ago, she began the fascinating art of creating designs using empty egg shells! She uses everything from large ostrich eggs to the tiniest of bird eggs, ordering them from various suppliers. She creates her own patterns and uses surgical instruments to carve intricate filigree designs that turn a simple eggshell into a collector's dream. Some of her largest shells are ornately decorated and can be opened to reveal a scene inside, a tiny music box or a velvet lining holding a smaller decorated egg.

Heather travels regularly to attend shows, sometimes teaching classes or participating in seminars. She says, "I have several extended families—the egg world, the quilters, and the crafters."

Her own family includes three children and several grandchildren.

Widowed twice, she has lived in Florida to be near one son and now lives in Missouri to be near her daughter. She has also traveled to visit her other son's family who live in Malaysia while he works in China.

In earlier years, she taught ceramics classes at a home for unwed mothers and was the activities director at a home for seniors. Today, she still teaches classes to seniors who live in her lovely independent living facility—and one of her students is 101 years old. When Heather is in Mexico, she teaches classes there too.

Heather's small apartment today is like a cozy museum filled with cabinets and shelves holding a variety of fabulous egg designs, a small collection of egg-head dolls with curly hair and handmade dresses, and a small collection of Mexican jewelry. She says, "I don't make money from all this but I just love doing all of it."

In spite of all her work, Heather appears very quiet and serene, happy with the life she has made for herself. But she does like to keep working. She says, "If a day passes and I have nothing to show that I have accomplished something—a new design, a bit of sewing, a class taught— I feel it is a wasted day."

Dear Lord, they say variety is the spice of life and Heather has certainly turned her retirement days into a delicious spicy recipe. I've noticed many seniors are happiest when they are able to continue, possibly in a limited fashion, to do what they always did!

Some continue to sew, knit, write, paint, travel, babysit, entertain friends, or have family gatherings. And others—bless them—spend their time helping or praying for others. Thank you, Lord, for the variety of ways seniors today are spicing up this "third stage of life," this new "Millionaire's Club."

Men go forth to wonder at the heights of mountains, the huge waves of the sea, the broad flow of the rivers, the vast compass of the ocean, the courses of the stars—and they pass by themselves without wondering. ST. AUGUSTINE

*G*od made all those wonders—and then he made you and me. Don't pass by yourself without wondering—and pondering. The later years are a gift—a time to pray more, love more, and even enjoy more; a time to get to know yourself better and to appreciate all of God's creations.

WOULD YOU LIKE
TO RIDE A CAMEL?

reg Harris liked to look ahead so he made a list of all the things he hoped to do when he retired. As soon as he was free from job commitments, he began checking off his senior to-do list. One thing he always wanted to do was to go see the pyramids and ride a camel. His budget never allowed him to do that but one Christmas, when there was a local nativity scene with live animals, they were offering camel rides. So, along with the children, he climbed up on a camel and felt like Lawrence of Arabia!

When some people retire, they think, "What do I do now?" Others have their list ready. Do you have a senior want-to-do list? If not, make up one now and start having some fun plus a sense of accomplishment as you check off the items on your list. Each person's list will be different but here a few suggestions:

☐ If you like animals, volunteer at an animal shelter. Most of them welcome senior volunteers with open arms—and so do the dogs and cats!

- ☐ If your town has a planetarium, check the schedule and go discover the universe.

- ☐ Join a book discussion club at a bookstore or library and meet new friends, or join a Scripture study club and meet new biblical friends.

- ☐ If your town has a water tower, find out if they allow visitors to climb up and get a whole new view of your area.

- ☐ If your town has a hotel that features a top-story restaurant, have lunch there and ask for a window seat to get a different view.

- ☐ Volunteer at a soup kitchen and see how some people make do when they are between jobs or homeless.

- ☐ Sign up to take a class at a community college.

- ☐ If you have a talent—knitting, cake decorating, French cooking, comfort cooking, computer-usage, woodworking, gardening, tutoring of any kind— start your own class. Maybe put a note on the church bulletin board advertising it or if you would not want people to come to your home, ask your pastor if you could start a class using a church facility.

- ☐ If you are good at making things—jewelry, flower pots, personalized note paper, "crafty" gift items— make up a batch and rent a booth at a local craft fair or church bazaar and find out if you might also be good at selling them!

☐ Get on the move! Sign up for a swim class, a yoga class, a cooking class, etc.—to give you something new to look forward to! And if you don't want to do this alone, ask a friend to sign up with you.

☐ Get involved! Volunteer to help with a political campaign, a local charity, or one of the organizations at your church or school. They are looking for helpers.

☐ If you're feeling weighed down, you might go on a diet but make it a spiritual experience. Pretend it's Lent, give up all high-calorie foods, and pray a lot! In a few weeks you could be a new you, ready to take on new retirement adventures.

☐ Volunteer to be an usher at a local theatre—meet new people and see all the shows for free!

☐ If you're a pet lover, you might make some money and get exercise at the same time by becoming a dog-walker!

☐ If you're musical, you could give music lessons in your home, make some spending money, and make some younger friends!

☐ If you love to garden, you could join—or start—a neighborhood garden club.

☐ Volunteer to house-sit for friends when they go away on business trips or vacations—water their flowers, feed their pets, etc.

☐ Sit in a garden or by a lake and think about all the blessings in your life. And make a list!

SENIORS
HELPING SENIORS

S ome seniors have lots of energy and time and are looking for useful retirement activities. Other seniors may have temporary or long-term disabilities that keep them from doing small jobs around the house that need attention. To solve both problems, some parishes are starting senior care teams. Volunteers gather to set up a file of names of people who volunteer to help and then they match each request for help with whoever has the time or ability to do the job. They welcome anyone who can give an hour a month as much as someone who is able to be "on call" most of the time. They are careful to not overcommit any member. It is a spiritual venture as well as an active one and the members of these teams find that they have been blessed abundantly by this give-and-take plan.

If your church doesn't have such an organization, maybe you could be the one to start one.

These are the kinds of jobs seniors have been helping with:

Simple home repairs

planting flowers

raking leaves

replacing difficult-to-reach light bulbs

running errands

dusting a room

mopping a floor

grocery shopping

giving a ride to a doctor's appointment

offering an hour off to a caretaker

taking a treat to a shut-in

dropping by or calling just for a chat

helping pack for a trip to visit relatives

helping a senior "downsize" and have a garage sale

These are simple activities that could make a big difference to someone who needs just a little bit of help to keep on keeping on!

"...Coming In on a Wing and a Prayer..."

*I*n 1943, during World War II, there was a song and/ or a story about a pilot who was coming back from a mission when he was attacked and his plane lost an engine. As he tried to make it back to base with only one engine and a full crew aboard, he sent a radio message that said "with trust in the Lord," he was "coming in on a wing and a prayer."

That seems an appropriate theme for those whose stories are told in this book—and for all of today's seniors—who, in very different and unique ways, are making the most of every day left of life and, with trust in the Lord, keeping in mind that they are "coming home with a laugh and a prayer."